T0032864

THE PERFECT DAY TO
BOSS UP

Also by Rick Ross with Neil Martinez-Belkin

Hurricanes: A Memoir

RICK ROSS

WITH NEIL MARTINEZ-BELKIN

THE PERFECT DAY TO
BOSS UP

A HUSTLER'S GUIDE TO BUILDING YOUR EMPIRE

HANOVER
SQUARE
PRESS

If you purchased this book without a cover you should be aware that this book is stolen property. It was reported as "unsold and destroyed" to the publisher, and neither the author nor the publisher has received any payment for this "stripped book."

**HANOVER
SQUARE
PRESS™**

Recycling programs
for this product may
not exist in your area.

ISBN-13: 978-1-335-47510-7

The Perfect Day to Boss Up

First published in 2021. This edition published in 2022 with revised text.

Copyright © 2021 by Rick Ross
Copyright © 2022 by Rick Ross, revised text edition

All rights reserved. No part of this book may be used or reproduced in any manner whatsoever without written permission except in the case of brief quotations embodied in critical articles and reviews.

This publication contains opinions and ideas of the author. It is intended for informational and educational purposes only. The reader should seek the services of a competent professional for expert assistance or professional advice. Reference to any organization, publication or website does not constitute or imply an endorsement by the author or the publisher. The author and the publisher specifically disclaim any and all liability arising directly or indirectly from the use or application of any information contained in this publication.

Hanover Square Press
22 Adelaide St. West, 41st Floor
Toronto, Ontario M5H 4E3, Canada
HanoverSqPress.com
BookClubbish.com

Printed in U.S.A.

TABLE OF CONTENTS

INTRODUCTION

THE FUNGUS WAS
AMONG US

I WAS ABOUT TO BOARD MY FLIGHT WHEN the gate agent approached me and asked if I would mind stepping to the side of the line. At first I didn't think anything of it. I figured she was trying to get herself a quick selfie with Rozay, and who could blame her for that? It's not every day that the biggest boss shows up at your workplace.

"I'm sorry to bother you, Mr. Roberts, but I have to ask. Are you and your party planning on staying in Colombia for the next sixty days?"

Now, I would love to kick off this book by telling you I was getting on a chartered jet to go procure a hundred kilos from a plug in Cartagena. But that would be a fabrication. I have to be honest. First of all, I was flying commercial that day, as I usually do. The PJs are nice for family vacations and romantic getaways, but when you fly as often as I do, the cost of flying private adds up quick. Flights are one of the few times

I'm able to get some sleep, so to spend all that extra when I'm just going to be getting my beauty rest always seems like a waste of money. First class treats me just fine. Anyway, the real reason I was headed to Colombia was to see my dentist, Dr. Mario Montoya. He was going to hook me up with a beautiful set of coke-white porcelain veneers.

"Did you say *sixty* days?" I asked. "I'm getting my billion-dollar smile and then I'm gone. You know I've got places to be."

"Oh... Okay... Well, if your billion smiles thing is an elective procedure, then we here at American Airlines strongly recommend that you consider postponing your trip. Due to the recent coronavirus outbreak, the United States may be temporarily closing its borders soon, and if that happens, there's a possibility you may not be able to reenter the country for a while."

I was confused. I was watching people scan their boarding passes and get on this flight. Then I realized we were the only Black people there. Everybody else looked Latino. This lady knew we weren't Colombians heading home, and I appreciated the racial profiling. She had just saved me from spending the next two months stuck in South America. I told the young woman she had a bright future in the airline industry and asked her to help me and my team retrieve our checked luggage from the plane. I broke her off with a few dollars for her troubles.

I had been hearing things about the coronavirus for a couple of weeks, and a few of my shows had gotten pushed back because of it. Originally the plan had been to fly from Colombia to Puerto Rico, where I was scheduled to perform at the Afro Nation Puerto Rico music festival the following week. But two days before my flight to Colombia, the event got canceled.

Recognizing the national concerns surrounding Covid-19 and under the instruction of the Puerto Rican Government, the Afro Nation organizers have announced that with much regret, they will not be going ahead with the festival due to take place in San Juan next week. Customers will be contacted in relation to refunds with details on rescheduling to come. If requested, refunds will be processed within seven working days.

Instead of heading back to my house in Davie, I had my sister book a block of rooms at the St. Regis Bal Harbour. I was thinking I'd treat my team to a few days of kicking it on the beach at my favorite hotel while this coronavirus situation got sorted out. Then I'd be back on my way to see Dr. Montoya and get my new teeth.

That's not how things played out. Over the next few days, it became increasingly clear that the coronavirus wasn't going away anytime soon. Whatever this shit was, we were nowhere near the end of it. The fungus was among us and it was just getting started.

The next morning, I got word that the iHeartRadio Music Awards, where I was nominated for Hip-Hop Song of the Year for "Money in the Grave" with Drake, would not be taking place. Then my Las Vegas residency at Mandalay Bay was suspended until further notice. Then the Funk Fest music festival in Orlando got postponed. Then Rolling Loud. At that point, I knew it was only a matter of time before they pulled the plug on my upcoming Feed the Streetz Tour. And sure enough, they did.

The health and safety of the fans, artists and staff are of the utmost importance during these times. We encourage everyone to comply with the directives of the local, state and national authorities to curb the rise of this very serious public health threat. We, along with our venue partners, apologize for the inconvenience but know that we are working tirelessly to provide all concertgoers with an unforgettable experience and safe environment.

Damn. We had just officially announced the tour, and I was super excited for it. It was shaping up to be one for the history books with an all-star lineup stacked with heavy hitters from the South: Jeezy, 2 Chainz, T.I., Yo Gotti, Lil' Kim, Boosie Badazz and DJ Drama.

And I was the headliner. Those shows were fitting to be so live and ghetto and project. I was looking forward to going city to city with those guys. That particular group was a crew of partiers, and we'd all known each other for over a decade. Between the concerts and the after-parties in every city we touched down in, I knew we were all going to have a lot of fun and make a lot of money that summer.

One by one, all of my plans for the remainder of the year fell out. In the blink of an eye, my 2020 calendar had been wiped clean. This Covid-19 shit was serious.

Now that this fungus was affecting my pockets— millions of dollars of expected revenue had just been taken off my table—I decided to educate myself on what exactly this coronavirus was. As soon as I started reading about the symptoms, I knew it was real bad. And I knew that because I'd realized that I'd already had coronavirus.

Three months earlier, on December 18, 2019, I had traveled to the Middle East for a pair of shows in Saudi Arabia and Dubai. Shout-out to Swizz Beatz for bringing me out there. From there I flew to South Africa, where I had three more dates lined up in Durban, East London and Mahikeng. But I didn't end up doing any of those shows. There was some issue with the promoters. That's a story for another day.

In hindsight, I must have caught a case of the Covid

on my way back to the States, because within a few days of being home, I was coming down with something. At first my symptoms were pretty mild. I had a slight fever and a dry cough. But as the days went on, my symptoms kept getting worse and worse, and by the end of the week, I was in rough shape.

I felt like I'd gotten hit by a truck, but I tried to boss up and muscle through it. I still went down to Miami for my show at Club LIV on January 3. I remember I had on a blue blazer that night. I had a joint in one hand and a big Cuban cigar in the other. But I was having so much trouble breathing that I ended up putting the weed out and just held up the cigar and a bottle of Luc Belaire for aesthetic purposes. It felt like for every ten breaths I took, only three of them were decent. Like I had to gasp for air. If I was sick to the point where I couldn't even smoke my joint, I knew I had a problem.

I had planned on flying back to Atlanta the next morning, but I was so fucked-up, I decided to stay in Miami for a couple more days. I've dealt with some major respiratory issues throughout my life, and I knew the heat and humidity of South Florida would help me recover sooner than I would in Atlanta. So I came up with a plan. I would hunker down at my crib until I beat whatever this shit was.

I went up to my bedroom and cut the air-conditioning off. I rubbed Vicks VapoRub on the soles of my feet, hiked my socks up and pulled my hoodie over my head. I placed a spit bucket next to my lounge chair and sat down. My breathing had gotten so bad that I couldn't sleep lying down. I had to be upright in order to get any air in my lungs. I put on *Forensic Files*—my favorite show—and waited. But when I started to cough, nothing was coming up. This wasn't like when I had bronchitis or pneumonia and I had all this fluid and mucus I needed to flush out of my system. This cough was so fucking hoarse and dry. I'd never experienced that before.

When my initial plan didn't work, I started to get a little concerned. I even hit up Tia and asked if she could swing by. Tia is my son Will's mother, and our issues over the years have been well publicized. But we had recently put our issues aside, and for the first time in years, we were co-parenting on good terms. Tia knows how to do facials and shit like that, so I asked if she could come through and put the humidifier in my face. As soon as she got to the house, she could see I wasn't right.

"I brought the humidifier, but I think you need to see a doctor," she said. "Will, you don't look like yourself."

The next day, I had a doctor come over. He wasn't sure exactly what was going on with me, but he gave me some pills to take and a vitamin B12 shot. As he was administering the shot, we heard a loud, nasty cough coming from the other room. It was my homeboy Skinny, and his cough sounded just like mine. The doctor gave me a concerned look.

"Do you know what's going on with him? Because whatever you've got, he has it too."

Once it hit me that the shit that had knocked me down for damn near a month back in January was this Covid-19 pandemic that was going on now, it was like a light bulb went off in my head. All of these strange observations I'd had the last three months suddenly started making sense.

On my way back from South Africa, I'd had a layover at Heathrow Airport in England. I remembered seeing a lot of people wearing face masks. At the time, I didn't think anything of it. I'd been seeing people wearing masks at the airport for years. But in retrospect, there were most definitely much more of them than usual. I guess they were already up on the fungus then. It wasn't on my radar yet.

I thought about that flight down to Miami before my show at LIV. I remembered seeing Skinny sleeping on that flight and finding that odd. Skinny doesn't really like to fly, and when he does, he's most definitely not falling asleep. My homie served twelve years in Polk CI, and he ain't been home long enough to where he can just comfortably knock out in a plane surrounded by strangers. Skinny be on high alert at all times. So I remembered being surprised seeing him sleeping.

At that point, I knew 2020 was over with. They were saying my Feed the Streetz Tour was going to be rescheduled for later that summer, but I didn't believe that. None of my dates were going to be rescheduled anytime soon. I didn't have to be an epidemiologist like Dr. Fauci to know that.

I needed to sit down and figure out a new play for 2020 given the drastic change in circumstances. Luckily I knew of the perfect place I could do that. I put on an N95 mask, checked out of the St. Regis and headed to the airport to get on the next flight to Atlanta. I was headed to The Promise Land.

CHAPTER

1

DETERMINE YOUR DESTINATION

THE PROMISE LAND IS MY 235-ACRE ESTATE located in Fayetteville, Georgia. There wasn't a better place on the planet for me to quarantine. I would have everything I could possibly need. I had a brand-new state-of-the-art recording studio where I could work on music. A home gym for my RossFit workouts. There's a movie theater. An arcade. A bowling alley. Indoor and outdoor basketball courts. A softball field. A horse stable. The largest residential swimming pool in the United States of America. And if the fungus spiraled out of control and turned into some type of zombie apocalypse situation, the 45,000-square-foot house had enough bedrooms to bring all my people and keep them safe. I was looking forward to spending an extended period of time at the estate. I hadn't spent more than a couple days at a time there since I bought it in 2014. I was always too busy.

A lot of my fans think I spend my days at The Promise Land surrounded by beautiful half-naked women who fan me with palm leaves and feed me pears. I can't say those people are lying. I do have days like that and I thoroughly enjoy them. But the truth is those days are the exception, not the rule. The public perception of my life is a little different than reality.

The reality of my life is that I work hard. I came in the rap game yelling, "Everyday I'm hustlin'," and that wasn't just the hook on a song. That was my real lifestyle. I wasn't lying then and shit ain't really changed much since. It's been fifteen years since the release of my breakout single and I still hustle hard every day. I may have a lot more cars in my garage and commas in my bank account, but the way I spend my time and move on a day-to-day basis has pretty much stayed the same.

For the last fifteen years, live performances have been my biggest source of income. When it comes to doing shows, I don't turn down a lot of bags. I'm on the road most weekends from Thursday through Sunday and I do it all. Stadiums. Music festivals. Club appearances. If you've got a budget for the boss and come correct with the numbers, I'm available for weddings, sweet sixteens and bar mitzvahs. I spend as many nights in hotels every year as I do in my own bed.

That's not out of the ordinary. Show money is the primary revenue stream for most artists. So when the fungus showed up and the show money disappeared overnight, I knew a lot of rappers were about to go broke. But Ricky Rozay is not most rappers. Show money is a big revenue stream, but it's still just one of many streams. Unlike a lot of these rappers, I don't keep all my Fabergé eggs in one basket. In case you haven't heard, Rozay is a serial entrepreneur with a diversified portfolio.

I am a multiplatinum-selling, Grammy-nominated recording artist. That's first and foremost. I am the founder of Maybach Music Group, home to Wale and Meek Mill. I own so many fast-food franchises, I've lost count of my exact number of locations. I'm in the wine and spirits industry. I have my own line of potato chips and ramen noodles. I'm the *New York Times* bestselling author of *Hurricanes: A Memoir*. I have a line of hair care and men's grooming products. I'm a partner in a sports agency. I rent my home out to the biggest film studios for major motion pictures. I own a cannabis company. The list goes on. By the time this book drops, I'll have several more ventures, so I apologize in advance to my future business partners for not shouting you out here. I'll get you in my next book.

What I'm saying is even if one part of my operation goes bust, which it did when the pandemic hit, the foundation was always going to stand strong regardless. This is why I call MMG the untouchable empire. This is why I'm going to be rich forever.

Still, when the fungus showed up, my whole way of life was turned upside down like everyone else. I wasn't tripping over the loss in show money. There were a lot of ways I could make that back. I was more curious about what I would do with all the new time I had on my hands. I needed to find me a new hobby.

My first quarantine purchase was a John Deere 5090E. It's a top-of-the-line utility tractor. I already owned a couple of zero-turn lawn mowers. A Z930 and a Z970R. I call those my shiteaters. The shiteaters are good for the edges and hard-to-reach spots by the ponds. But The Promise Land is too big to get everything done on the shiteaters. If I was going to start cutting my grass during this lockdown, then I needed the climate-controlled cab of the 5090E. Georgia summers get too hot for a rich, handsome fat nigga to be out in the sun for hours sweating like a pig. I couldn't allow all the people driving by my house to see me like that when I cut my grass. I have a reputation as an international sex symbol to uphold. I needed the air-conditioning and I needed the tinted windows.

Most of my vehicle purchases are considered liabilities. I'm talking about my Rolls-Royces and my Maybachs and my Ferraris, just to name a few. Those are acquisitions that have depreciated in value since I bought them. I have a lot more assets than liabilities, but I never said I was perfect. We all have our vices, and one of mine is most definitely my cars. I blame my so-called "friends" who sell me these automobiles. Every other week they show up to my crib unannounced with a beautiful new car knowing damn well that that's my weakness and I won't be able to say no. I say shame on these people for enabling my addiction. But this tractor didn't fall into that category. This was a guilt-free purchase because this was going to be an asset.

Before it became The Promise Land, my estate was previously known as Villa Vittoriosa, aka "The Victory." That was the name given to it by its original owner, four-time world heavyweight boxing champion Evander "The Real Deal" Holyfield. But when I purchased the estate at auction for $5.8 million, I didn't buy it from Evander Holyfield. I bought it from JPMorgan Chase & Co. The bank had bought the house for $7.5 million a few years earlier as part of a foreclosure. Despite having earned hundreds of millions of dollars over the course of his boxing career, the former champ had gone broke.

As I see it, several factors contributed to Holyfield losing his fortune. There were failed business ventures that didn't align with his brand. There were incompetent financial advisers and greedy fight promoters who lined their pockets. There were many reasons. But one of them was this house. According to Holyfield, he put $20 million into building the estate. But by the time he got it up and running, his boxing career was coming to an end. As he aged out of his prime and his paydays became less and less, he could no longer keep up with the high costs of maintaining Villa Vittoriosa.

If I didn't want to suffer the same fate as Holyfield, I had to make different types of moves. They say the definition of insanity is doing the same thing over and over again and expecting different results. Take a good long look at my face. Do I look crazy to you?

For starters, as long as I was stuck at home, I was going to be cutting my grass. Holyfield reportedly owed more than $500,000 to a landscaping company when he lost the house. That wasn't going to be me. If I had all the machinery and equipment, then I was my own landscaping company. I could hire my own people at a fraction of the cost of outsourcing all the work. Buying this tractor was me cutting out the middleman. It might take a few years before I started seeing the ROI—return on investment—but in the long run, this purchase was going to save me money. My motto is that if it ain't a long-term play, then it's just small talk.

I rolled me a few swishers and brought them with me inside the tractor. I cranked it up, lit my joint, and I was off to the races. As I began roaming the property, I realized how much of it I still hadn't properly explored. I was always too busy. Now I was getting acquainted with all of the fine details of The Promise Land. The pink flowers blooming from the eastern redbud trees. The anthills. The little brown mushrooms. I took a photo of them and texted my forager plug to find out if they would make me hallucinate. Maybe a psychedelic experience was what I needed right now. But he hit me back and told me they were useless russula. The weed was going to have to be enough for me today.

One thing I wasn't happy about was all the goose shit. These motherfuckers were shitting everywhere. I considered going back to the house and grabbing a rifle so I could send them a clear message but decided I would deal with them another day. I was offended the geese would defecate so recklessly all over The Promise Land. I thought the geese and I were cool. Whatever happened to good manners?

I rode out to the stable and fed apples and carrots to my three horses. I used to have four, but one of them had recently passed away. I wanted to get a new one. Off-white with dark brown patches. I believe they call those pinto horses. I made up my mind that once I turned in my next album, I was going to treat myself to a pinto.

I went to the back of the house and got out to sit on the swing by the pond. I wondered what the months ahead would bring. This pandemic was no joke. Things were probably going to be very different for a while. How would I handle that? As I stared out into the water, the words of the late, great Bruce Lee, from his short-lived TV show *Longstreet*, came to mind.

Empty your mind. Be formless, shapeless, like water.
When you pour water in a cup, it becomes the cup.
When you pour water in a teapot, it becomes the teapot.
Water can flow or drip or crash. Be water, my friend.

Bruce Lee knew what the fuck he was talking about. I was going to be like water. No matter what challenges this pandemic presented, I was going to go with the flow and adjust accordingly. I was going to find ways to win regardless.

I thought about getting into the pedal boat that was docked by the pond. Then I thought better of it. I might fuck around and sink the Sun Dolphin 5. Imagine if they found the boss floating facedown in the water. I couldn't go out like that.

I hopped back in the tractor and headed toward the softball field. Roberts Field. I'd gotten a dope custom scoreboard with my face on it when I first bought the estate, but I'd barely gotten any use out of it. What else could I do here?

I stood at home plate and analyzed the slope of the hill. Then it hit me. The softball diamond would be a perfect place for an amphitheater. I could host summer concerts where I could showcase up-and-coming artists I was working with. Or invite some comedians and have stand-up comedy nights at the estate. I'm talking some real intimate, exclusive player shit.

The only problem with that idea was that home plate marked the end of the property, and there were a few other homes nearby. I knew the Fayette County Sheriff's Office was just waiting for someone to put out a noise complaint against me. Read my first book if you want to know about my experiences interacting with them. But I also knew the eighty-seven acres behind The Promise Land had been up for sale for a while. They were asking $1.7 million, but if I could talk them down to a million, I might do it. I could do a lot with an additional eighty-seven acres.

I finally ran out of gas in front of the white barn that sits next to my guesthouse. I'd also run out of weed, so it was a good time for me to take a break anyway. I checked my phone and couldn't believe how late it was. I'd been out on the tractor for hours. I've never meditated before, but this was what I imagined that must feel like. I was present, living in the moment, free from all of my usual distractions and obligations. It had resulted in all these new observations and fresh ideas. At a time when the whole world was on standby and nothing was happening, it was becoming clear what things needed to happen. There's something centering about riding a tractor at a low speed for a few hours. I needed to do this more often.

The last time I was confined to my house like this was in 2015 when I was on house arrest. That period of solitude brought out a different side of me too. You can hear it in my music from that time in songs like "Foreclosures," "Free Enterprise" and "Smile Mama, Smile." But this time around was different. Back in 2015, I remember going stir-crazy. I knew that outside the gates of The Promise Land, everything was business as usual, and that I was the only one living under lockdown. There were moves to be made and I was the only one missing out on them. This time the whole world was on pause. I wasn't missing out on shit. There was something liberating about that.

I remembered briefly checking out the barn when I first took a tour of the estate, but that was six years ago, and I hadn't been inside there since. The truth was I'd pretty much forgotten all about it. When I stepped out of the tractor, I noticed a gold sign above the front entrance. The lettering reminded me of the Death Row Records logo.

REAL DEAL RECORDS

Right.

That's what this barn was. After Holyfield retired from boxing, he had tried to get into the music game, and this had been his label's headquarters. Remember when I told you about his business ventures that didn't really line up with his brand? Real Deal Records had been one of those.

But when I opened the door and went inside, I remembered what this barn really was. The walls were lined with mirrors, and there was the outline of a large square in the center of the room, where a boxing ring had once stood. Before this barn was Real Deal Records, this had been Holyfield's old gym. This was where he had trained for his title fights against the greats of his era, like Mike Tyson, Lennox Lewis and Buster Douglas. I could tell you where I watched every one of those fights.

What could I do with *this* space? I had the new studio being built in the main house, so the abandoned recording setup here would have to go. I was probably going to have to gut the barn. Then what? What if I turned it into a full-fledged production studio?

For years I'd wanted to launch a Maybach Films division. I'd been ahead of the curve when it came to creating daily online content for the hip-hop blogs. Back in '09, me and my videographer Spiff TV shot visuals every day on his DSLR camera. By the next morning, we'd have something new posted on World-StarHipHop.

I had always wanted to take our production value to the next level. But again, I was just always too busy running around to focus on a big undertaking like that. Now that I was stuck at home for the foreseeable future, I had the time and space to take that on. I closed my eyes and tried to imagine the RED cameras, lighting grids and green screens in here. I thought about installing a steel mezzanine to double up the available floor space. I could make this happen. I was going to make this happen.

It was surreal that this piece of boxing history belonged to me, but what was really fucking me up was that it had just occurred to me now for the first time.

I'd owned this barn for six years. How had I never thought about what I could do with it?

For the last few years, my main focus had been pushing my net worth past the $100 million mark. I was damn near there. I'd said yes to every promoter who wanted to book me and every opportunity to do a paid guest verse. I'd been relentless promoting all the brands in my portfolio. I'd enjoyed every minute of it. But I'd had to make sacrifices. Quality time with my kids. Enjoying the fruits of my labor at the estate. My health. I always told myself I'd be able to focus more on those things once I hit nine figures.

When you are chasing something, you can develop tunnel vision. It's a gift and a curse. On the one hand, it can be the fastest way to get you where you want to go and the easiest way to tune out all distractions. But it can also be a trap. The downside of tunnel vision is you can lose sight of everything else that's going on around you. And there is always more to life than any singular thing you're chasing. The goal is to strike a balance between having blinders on with no peripheral vision and being overstimulated and distracted by everything that's going on to the point that you can't get anything done.

One of my favorite books is Robert Greene's cult classic *The 48 Laws of Power*. Even though Robert wrote a book with 50 Cent, I'm still a fan of his work, and I've learned a lot from reading his books. But I never completely agreed with all of the laws. When I had the opportunity to meet Robert, I told him so. He reminded me that every law has a reversal, and that sometimes you need to do the opposite depending on the circumstances and the situation.

The pandemic was a perfect example of that. For fifteen years, I put so much of my time and energy toward getting to the money on the road. And for fifteen years, that was the play. But all of a sudden, I had to figure out a new play. Live performances were gone, and nobody knew when they were coming back or what they were going to look like when they did. So I had to reevaluate how I was allocating my time and attention and what I should be focusing on. By all means, when you're working toward something, you need to concentrate on the task at hand. That's when having tunnel vision is effective. But the best quarterbacks don't just see the wide receiver they plan to throw the ball to. They see every player and opportunity on the field.

There's not a one-size-fits-all approach to success. A boss has the ability to see the bigger picture and adjust their plans as their circumstances and their priorities evolve. Sometimes you have to take a step back and reassess to make sure you're still heading in the right direction. I had to do that in response to the fungus. When you can't make sense of what you're seeing, don't stare harder. When you're confused by what you're hearing, don't listen harder. Stand back, give yourself some space and let things come into focus.

I wasn't sure what the future had in store for me, but I knew that I was going to make something of it. I wasn't going to let this extra time go to waste. Somehow, someway, I was going to figure out how to be even more successful during the pandemic than I would have been otherwise. Maybe the fungus would turn out to be a blessing in disguise for Rozay. Maybe this was the perfect day to boss up.

CHAPTER

2

THE GAME AIN'T
BASED ON SYMPATHY

I COULD HAVE JUSTIFIED TAKING THE REST of the year off. I could have accepted the fact that I was going to take a financial loss in 2020, and who could have blamed me for that? It wasn't my fault the fungus showed up like the Grinch on Christmas Eve and stole all the money bags I had lined up. I had a good excuse to lose, right? Maybe so. But the game ain't based on sympathy. The government wasn't cutting Rozay any PPP checks just because my Vegas residency got canceled. So tell me how my good excuse was going to benefit me?

Were you able to come up with something? I wasn't. But I was able to come up with plenty of ways I could offset the loss of show money. For one, I could lock myself in the studio and knock out as many guest verses as it took. The last time I checked, my features were still in high demand.

Grew up having nothing, you're labeled impatient
But once the boss made it, you're labeled amazing

Meticulous with words, that's your force of nature
I don't wanna seem absurd, but that boy's a gangster

—Anderson .Paak feat. Rick Ross, "Cut Em In,"
Madden NFL 21 Soundtrack (2020)

A petty problem have your ass doin' thirty years
But her future bright, it's time to touch these thirty M's
Cocaine and Maybachs throughout the catalog
Expensive heels for pretty bitches, I had 'em all

—Rick Ross feat. Bryson Tiller, "Future Bright,"
Bad Boys for Life Soundtrack (2020)

She sees just how I ride and slip her panties off
He wanted war until they hit 'em with a cannonball
Spark spliffs, raw kicks I get from Clark Kent
Common sense, no prints, strictly the mob hits

—Freddie Gibbs feat. Rick Ross, "Scottie Beam,"
Alfredo (2020)

All I wanna do is see the real niggas be rewarded
Fuck a bag, go and buy a whole city for my daughter
Big homie sixty-five still doing time, that's in the feds
What's the use climbing to the mountaintop if you living
on the ledge

—Jeezy feat. Rick Ross, "Almighty Black Dollar,"
The Recession 2 (2020)

Count your acres, build your estates, we call it farm life

Talkin' heavy, your chains sound hollow when your charm
light

Pistol poppin', your whip look polished and your broad's
nice

Kemosabe, hundred kilos just on a calm night

> —T.I. feat. Rick Ross, "Respect the Code,"
>
> *The L.I.B.R.A.* (2020)

Niggas desire to fit in, I was invited

Pistol-whipped a few niggas, he got indicted

When you face a few years, it's time to fight it

I shook the prosecutor right back, Johnny Unitas

> —Benny the Butcher feat. Rick Ross,
>
> "Where Would I Go," *Burden of Proof* (2020)

Silk fleeces, Jesus pieces

Here's my memoir, I need your thesis

After I've read chapter five

In the twenty-six, still side by side

> —Skip Marley feat. Rick Ross and Ari Lennox,
>
> "Make Me Feel," *Higher Place* (2020)

Watches set in baguettes, in my Champion sweats

I got four or five jewelers, I just purchase the wet

Now the bottle's all black, no more sipping Moët

Dropped the top, bump "The Woo," show the tats on
   my chest

> —Curren$y feat. Rick Ross, "Mugello Red,"
> *The OutRunners* (2020)

I done seen a couple niggas lose they life over a dollar
And it hit the hardest when it's not an outsider
Better keep your money close 'cause that's the only thing
   that's honest
Everybody thuggin' 'til they gotta face your honor

> —Joyner Lucas feat. Rick Ross, "Legend,"
> *EVOLUTION* (2020)

That was light work. Too easy. I could knock out a
few of those every day. What else could I do? I could
go twice as hard at promoting my brands on social
media. I could hit up my old publishing partners at
Hanover Square Press and tell them to open up the
budget and cut the check because the biggest boss was
ready to bless them another *New York Times* bestseller.
So that's exactly what I did.

That's how this book was born. Instead of sitting at
home twiddling my thumbs waiting for things to go
back to how they were, I decided to take the obstacle
in front of me and turn it into an opportunity. I could
pull back the curtain on my success as a music mogul
and entrepreneur. I could share how I became the biggest boss and inspire someone to become the CEO of

their life. I could share the principles I've lived by that got me to where I'm at today. The Boss Commandments, if you will. I could drop some gems on these motherfuckers. Better yet, I could drop some diamonds.

The way I saw it, there were still plenty of opportunities for me to have a productive and prosperous 2020 in spite of the pandemic, and none of those opportunities involved me having a good excuse not to.

The dangerous part of excuses is that a lot of them make sense. The bank might not give you a loan to get your small business idea off the ground. You might not have any contacts in the media to help you promote your mixtape. You might not have the resources to service a record to radio independently. But you've still got to find a way. Stop looking for someone else to solve your problems for you. Nobody owes you shit.

At the end of the day, a legitimate excuse and a bad excuse serve the same purpose: to justify failure and minimize the amount of shame we feel for not figuring out a way to overcome the obstacles in our way.

As valid as an excuse might seem, it doesn't mean shit. Why not? Because Michael Jordan still dropped 38 points to win Game Five of the 1997 NBA Finals when he was sick with the flu. Tiger Woods still won the 2008 US Open on a broken leg. Tom Brady and the New England Patriots still came back to beat the Atlanta Falcons when they were down 28–3 in the third quarter of Super Bowl LI. The greats all had good excuses to lose too. But what separates the greats from the average is that they don't take the bait of a good excuse. They know that's the easy way out.

The only reason anyone even remembers that Jordan had the flu or that Tiger's leg was fucked-up is because they went out and won anyway. That's the only reason anybody knows about the excuses they could have used.

Your goals don't give a fuck about your excuses. Nobody gives a fuck about your excuses besides you. I promise you no one else cares or wants to hear that shit. So you can either wrap yourself up with your good excuses and pray they keep you warm at night, or you can find a way to win with the cards you were dealt. I'm not a boss because I had the perfect circumstances to boss up handed to me on a silver platter. I'm a boss because no matter how my circumstances conspired against me, I still went out and won. If you're waiting on your perfect opportunity to be presented to you in a gift-wrapped box with a red bow on top before pursuing your goals, you better find yourself a nice leather recliner and get comfortable because you're going to be sitting in that bitch waiting for the rest of your miserable life.

That moment you're waiting on doesn't exist. Everybody has problems and some people overcome them and other people use them as excuses. The way you choose to respond to your problems will have a greater impact on your success than the problems themselves.

Fuck a pandemic. To me, a global pandemic is just another opportunity. It's the perfect time to boss up.

What are your goals? One month from now you can either have made a month's worth of progress toward them or you can have a month's worth of excuses why you haven't done shit. At the end of the day, you're going to have to make a decision. Are you going to be a donkey or a bronco? Which one is it going to be?

CHAPTER

3

EVERY BOSS STARTED
OUT A WORKER

YOUR CHECKING ACCOUNT'S AVAILABLE balance is not what determines whether or not you're a boss. Being a boss is about being in the driver's seat of your life, regardless of whether you're riding in a Bugatti or your momma's Ford Focus. A lot of motherfuckers spend their whole lives sitting on the passenger side, passively accepting to go wherever their life takes them. A boss grabs a hold of the steering wheel and takes their life where they want to go.

When I see someone who has a vision, a road map to reach that destination and the heart to persevere through adversity, I see a boss. It doesn't matter if they're at square one. That individual has what it takes to reach their goals.

In my memoir, I wrote about a time during the early days of my rap career when I spent months living in DJ Greg Street's basement in Stone Mountain, Georgia. I was so broke at the time, my momma was covering my car payments so that my truck wouldn't get repossessed. When I would go out of town, I would sleep in my truck because I didn't have money to stay in a hotel.

I had a lot of people hit me after reading the book

because they couldn't believe what I'd written was true. This was when I first started networking and building relationships in the music industry. During those trips out of town when I would sleep in my car, I was also meeting and kicking it with certified hip-hop legends, like Tony Draper, J. Prince and Scarface. So a lot of these people who met me back then were shocked when they read about how broke and fucked-up I was because they never viewed me as the struggling college dropout I was when we first met. They viewed me then the same way people see me now. Like a boss. The way you carry yourself and the energy you project to the world play a major part in your success.

Look at Drake. My homie is damn near the top-selling musical artist of all time. But when I first met Drizzy, he was just the little homie of "The Best Rapper Alive," aka Lil Wayne. I remember when Weezy signed Drake to Young Money and started bringing him down to Miami. It really wasn't that long ago. A lot of motherfuckers didn't know what to make of a Black Jew from Canada who was rapping *and* singing. Nobody was on that wave then. Drake barely had a buzz when he and I first met, but I knew I was looking at a young boss in the making. It takes a lot of confidence to bring something new to the table the way he was doing.

Drake hadn't even released his first album when I decided to feature him on "Aston Martin Music," the third single off my fourth album, *Teflon Don*. "Aston Martin Music" ended up being the biggest hit on the album and my first single to go double platinum. Ever since then, whenever Drake blesses me a verse or a hook, that's a guaranteed plaque. He's been hip-hop's biggest hitmaker for over a decade. But I still remember when he started getting his first magazine covers and he would take pride in the fact that he had a stamp of approval from Rozay.

There's a difference between carrying yourself like a boss because you believe in yourself and being a fraudulent con artist trying to dupe people into thinking you're something that you're not. I saw an article the other day about a new business that charges aspiring social media influencers to take pictures of themselves in a fake private jet. I'm not talking about a real plane that's grounded in a hangar. What I'm talking about is a photography studio with a set made to look like the inside of a PJ. Now, I salute the young entrepreneurs who identified the market for this and are getting money. I don't knock their hustle. In fact, I want to give them some free game. I think they could charge more if they hire models to dress up as fake flight attendants that bring fake drinks to their fake passengers. But to the people who pay for these services, I think you should take an honest look at yourself and ask the tough question: Are you more concerned with looking successful than actually becoming successful?

To me, any type of fugazi shit like that is the definition of hustling backward. That's not the way you build an empire. That's how you build a house of cards. You don't become famous and then become great at something. Greatness is the thing that leads to money, status and, eventually, real chartered jets. I never invested my time, energy and resources into portraying a fake image of myself. I woke up every morning and put my blood, sweat and tears into turning my dreams into reality.

These days a lot of motherfuckers want to start the marathon at the finish line and be a boss without having to put the work in. They want instant gratification. I swear social media has fucked people's minds up bad. You scroll through IG and you see all these beautiful pictures, but you have to know that you're not getting the full picture. What you're looking at is the finished product. People become too obsessed with the finished product when they should be obsessed with the process that leads to the champagne corks popping. The process ain't as cool to look at. But you can't become successful by posting a picture that gets you a million likes. Success is the outcome of what you do when no one's paying attention to you. If you want to be a boss, you first have to be a worker.

CHAPTER

EMPIRES ARE BUILT
BRICK BY BRICK

Self-made, you just affiliated
I built it ground up, you bought it renovated
—Rick Ross feat. Styles P, "B.M.F.," *Teflon Don* (2010)

I HAVE OVER A DOZEN BUSINESS VENTURES and I want to tell you about all of them. But not yet. Because I couldn't branch out and have all of these irons in the fire until I mastered one thing first. For me that was making music. For you it could be anything. But you can't be successful at many things until you've figured out how to be successful at one thing first. You don't want to be a jack-of-all-trades and a master of none. You have to narrow your focus when you're starting out. Empires are built one brick at a time.

No matter how big your dream is—and I encourage everyone to let their imaginations run wild—you have to start small. You also have to come up with a game plan. Blind faith and wishful thinking won't get you anywhere, and neither will running around like a chicken with its head cut off trying to make something happen without a proper plan in place. Being active doesn't translate to being effective or productive. If your goal is to catch fish, the play isn't to run into the ocean and see how many of them you can grab with your hands. The play is to spend your time building yourself a fishing rod first. It might take a little longer before you're out on the water, but in the long run, you're going to catch a lot more fish than the caveman motherfucker trying to hunt with his bare hands. Before you can earn, you have to learn. The best piece of advice I ever got came from a mentor of mine by the name of Big Mike. Mike was a highly respected hustler, and coming up in Miami, the hustlers were who we looked up to. They drove the nicest cars, wore the flyest clothes and pulled the baddest hoes. So from an early age, I was trying to convince Mike to put me on. But for many years he turned me away and he always gave me the same reason.

"You gotta have game if you want to get work."

As a youngster, I couldn't really understand what Mike was trying to tell me. I was just pissed that I had a direct line on the plug and he wasn't letting me in on what he had going on. It wasn't until I got older that I was able to process what he was saying. I wasn't ready to be touching major weight. I didn't know a thing about entrepreneurship in the streets. How was Mike supposed to trust me to take bricks out of state before I'd proved that I was capable of holding my own, selling nicks and dimes in the Matchbox Projects around the corner from my house?

Having game is having knowledge. You acquire knowledge through learning. Learn the step-by-step process of working your way up the ladder in your chosen study. Study the moves of the ones who did it before you and learn from their stories. Mike was just one of my many mentors. Shout-out to my high school football coach Walt Frazier. Shout-out to Kenneth Williams. Shout-out to Tony Draper, J. Prince, Puff Daddy and Jay-Z. The list goes on. My OGs blessed me with a lot of game.

Once you've acquired enough game, you'll be ready to get to work. That's when you'll start to get some experience under your belt. Focus on sharpening your skills and mastering technique. Invest in your development and build your value up. Don't worry about money yet. That part comes later. When you become a specialist at something, the money will start to come to you.

Set goals for yourself that are ambitious and challenge you but also feel attainable. Ones that feel within reach. Be sure to take a moment to recognize and celebrate your small victories along the way. Success is a long journey, and acknowledging your progress will give you sustenance and keep you from burning out. With each step up the ladder, you'll be a little bit closer to that bigger vision.

The "10,000-Hour Rule," based on a study by Anders Ericsson and made popular by Malcolm Gladwell in his 2008 book *Outliers* theorizes that the key to success in any field is putting in 10,000 hours of practice.

In Gladwell's case, he claims to have hit that number with twenty hours of work a week for ten years.

That math makes sense to me. I graduated high school in 1994. A year later, I made the decision to walk away from my football scholarship at Albany State University and pursue my dream of becoming a rapper. Ten years later, just shy of my thirtieth birthday, I got my big break with "Hustlin'."

The "10,000-Hour Rule" ain't an exact science. To me, it's more of a metaphor of the amount of commitment it requires to excel at something. I can tell you from experience that the decade I spent working in the shadows is what prepared me for all the success I've had since.

"Hustlin'" wasn't my lucky break. It was the culmination of everything I'd learned in the ten years leading up to it. When I was starting out, I rapped totally differently. My raps were much more complex. My flow was faster. Back then I would have never thought to rhyme *Atlantic* with *Atlantic* like I did on "Hustlin'."

I was rapping my ass off, but I got no love for that hyper lyrical shit. It was only through those disappointments that I learned that most hit records have very simple melodies and repetitive hooks. I didn't have to perform lyrical acrobats. That's what made me switch my approach to writing raps and making records.

Let's take that a step further. How was I able to switch my whole style? I was able to do that because

I'd spent so many years ghostwriting for other artists. I'd rapped from so many different perspectives. I'd tried out so many different flows. Through years of trial and error, I figured out what worked. I got better and better.

When I became the subject of a major label bidding war, I knew what I wanted out of a record deal. How did I know? I knew because I'd already had two failed deals at Suave House and Slip-N-Slide Records. Are you following my logic? When you're putting in those first 10,000 hours, you're probably not going to get rich or famous. But you're going to slowly learn how to get those things.

I'm not going to lie to you. Those early years in the trenches consist of a lot of pain and sacrifice. Those are going to be the lean years when you put in a lot of blood, sweat and tears and get very little in return. But you have to play that position to get the promotion. This is how you go from muddy waters to marble floors.

There are people who buy their first lottery ticket and go from being broke to millionaires overnight. And there are people who write their first song and two weeks later it goes number one on the *Billboard* Hot 100. Those things do happen. But I don't consider those things true success. That's closer to hitting a lick or robbing the plug, if you ask Rozay. Any nigga can get lucky and win a ticket in a dice game. Very few can put up those types of wins consistently over an extended period of time.

In my experience, when someone's rise to the top is quick and easy, a hard and fast fall is usually right around the corner. Statistics back that up. Studies show that most lottery winners are back to where they started within a few years of receiving a large financial windfall. It makes sense. If you haven't really learned what it takes to earn a million, how are you supposed to know how to keep making millions?

Try to embrace the process. Believe it or not, you don't want it to be easy. When you've earned every ounce of your success, it makes it that much sweeter. My homie Brett likes to say that "Being self-made tastes better." There's more value in accomplishments that you earn than rewards that are given to you for free. Money, fame and prestige come and go, but when you put in the work and become great at something, nobody can ever take that away from you. You get to keep that forever.

CHAPTER

5

DON'T WASTE
YOUR TIME

THE QUARANTINE WAS A GOOD OPPORTU-nity for me to tackle some long-overdue spring clean-ing at The Promise Land. Despite the fact that my walk-in closet is bigger than most New York City apartments, it had exceeded capacity. I'd already had to sacrifice one of my guest rooms to make room for all my clothes and sneakers. I had plenty of guest rooms to spare, but if I didn't get this situation under control, I knew the producers at A&E were going to show up with the cameras and stage an intervention on Rozay for the next season of *Hoarders*. I couldn't go out like that. I needed to go through all of my shit and figure out what I could give away.

One thing in my closet that wasn't going anywhere was my watch box. My collection of timepieces means as much to me as my cars. When I opened up the case, it brought back a lot of memories. There were my Rolexes: the Oyster Perpetuals, Datejusts and Sky-Dwellers. I wish I still had that iced-out Rollie Tony Draper gave me when I first signed to Suave House. That was my first Rolex.

There were my Hublots: my limited-edition Dwyane Wade Big Bang and the one Dr. Dre gave me at my thirty-sixth birthday party at Club Amnesia. My Vacheron Constantin and the Audemars Piguet Royal Oak Offshore T3 that Arnold Schwarzenegger wore in *Terminator 3*. Once things opened back up, I needed to go see Jacob the Jeweler in New York. I had my sights set on one of his "Billionaire" watches.

Last night I cried tears of joy
What did I do to deserve this?
Vacheron on my wrist
A year ago I didn't even know the bitches exist
Quarter milli for the motherfucker
No insurance on the motherfucker

—Rick Ross feat. CeeLo, "Tears of Joy,"
Teflon Don (2010)

I like watches because they represent the most precious resource on earth. I'm not talking about diamonds, gold or platinum. I'm talking about time. The contents of my watch box may be worth millions, but time is truly priceless. It's the only thing in this world you can never get more of, regardless of how much paper you get. That means that how you choose to spend your time is the most important decision you will ever have to make.

I don't waste my time. I rise and grind every day. If you're somehow under the impression that what you do with your time doesn't directly determine your future, that's something you're going to have to figure out before you can successfully move forward with anything in life.

Regardless of your position, you have to think like a boss. Even if you feel like you're at the bottom of the food chain and there's no one underneath you. Even in that case, you still have to be the boss of yourself.

One thing that all bosses do is conduct performance reviews. So when you make the decision to become the CEO of your life, you have to be able to assess yourself objectively. You have to be self-aware. What are your areas of strength? What are your weaknesses? When you're drawing up your master plan, take inventory of all the resources at your disposal. What are you bringing to the table, and what are the ones that need to get brought? Most important, how effectively are you spending your time?

Since time is the most precious resource there is, time management and resource allocation go hand in hand. Let me break it down for you like this. Every day you get twenty-four hours to spend. This ain't an AT&T Rollover Minutes type of situation where if you're a lazy motherfucker one day and don't get shit done, you get to save those minutes and spend them better tomorrow instead. You don't get back wasted time. Once it's gone, it's gone forever.

Take out a pen and paper and jot down all the things you spend your time and attention on on a daily basis. I'm talking weekdays and weekends. A lot of people have to pursue their passion on nights and weekends, outside of the five-day, nine-to-five work schedule, in order to provide for their families and put food on the table. Ain't nothing wrong with that. But it makes it even more important that you audit how you spend your time.

Write it all down. The good things and the not-so-great things. Your day job. Your side hustle. Pursuing your education. Your hobbies. Your relationships. Exercising. Sleeping in. Hitting the clubs on Friday and Saturday nights. Netflix. Scrolling through your ex's IG and posting subliminal messages to your story to get their attention. Once you've covered all the activities, break down how much time you spend on each. Remember you only have twenty-four hours each day. Be honest with yourself about how you're spending your time and what is taking up your attention. Are you putting too much energy into things that aren't getting you closer to your goals? Don't bullshit me because I'm not going to be looking at your fucking worksheet. If you choose to lie to yourself, well, like my brother DJ Khaled says, "Congratulations, you played yourself."

After you've completed the exercise, do it again. But this time, close your eyes and visualize the best version of yourself. The one who stays on point and does what they're supposed to be doing day in and day out. The one who gets the absolute most out of their twenty-four hours. Not the lazy motherfucker version of you. I'm talking about the upgraded biggest boss version. How does that person spend their time each day? What trade-offs and sacrifices are they willing to make? When you compare the two breakdowns side by side, it starts to become clear where you're handling your business and where you may need to tighten up. The lifestyle changes you need to make. The bad habits you have to cut out. Or the people you might need some distance from. You need to have a clear sense of who you are and who you want to become in order to determine the changes you need to make. And then you need to hold yourself accountable and execute those changes. If you aren't willing to make changes, you shouldn't expect your situation to change.

> *What separates great players from all-time great players is their ability to self-assess, diagnose weaknesses and turn those flaws into strengths.*
>
> —Kobe Bryant

As long as you're spending your time wisely, try not to focus too much on what time it is. I know you've heard the expression "Rome wasn't built in a day." The idea is to remain patient when you're working toward your goals because all great things take time. People get confused and think hustling hard means moving fast. You don't need to move fast. You need to move correctly. Sometimes the heaviest tank on the battle-field moves the slowest.

I wouldn't go so far as to say I've got a bad album in my catalog, but numbers don't lie and I have my best-performing album and I have my worst-performing album. Going off that, the closest I've come to drop-ping a dud was when I rushed my creative process and released two albums in one year. I've always prioritized quality over quantity, but there were extenuating cir-cumstances at the time. Meek Mill had gotten locked up for a probation violation, and his highly anticipated sophomore album, *Dreams Worth More Than Money*, had to get pushed back. As the leader of MMG, I tried to step up for the team and put some numbers on the board in the fourth quarter by dropping another album. But there was a price to pay for rushing my creative process. When *Hood Billionaire* dropped in 2014, I saw the lowest first-week sales of my career. The reviews from critics weren't great either. The frustrating part was that that album had so much potential. It had so many dope ideas and concepts, and I knew that if I'd taken the necessary time to meticulously fine-tune and perfect that same track list of songs, the way I normally do, the response would have been much different. You can't rush greatness.

I know remaining patient is easier said than done.

Especially when you've been waiting on something a long time and you want it real bad. Believe me, I've been there. If you're like me, "Rome wasn't built in a day" probably isn't going to give you much peace of mind. If Rome wasn't built in a day, well, then I need to know how many fucking days that shit took. Unfortunately, I can't answer that for you. You're going to have to look that one up in a history book.

I most definitely can't tell you how long it will take you to reach your goals. Every come-up has its own timeline. So as best as you can, try not to get too hung up on when everything is going to come together. Concentrate on *what* is coming together. I might not be able to tell you how long it takes to build an empire, but I already told you how all empires are built. By getting up every day and laying bricks. The "when" part is up to God, and he has his own master plan that's more complicated than you or I could even begin to understand. You've got to trust that he always knows what he's doing, even during your darkest moments when it feels like he may have forgotten about you.

The closest I ever came to giving up on my dream was right before it finally came true. I remember the specific moment vividly. This must have been 2003 or 2004. I'd driven up to Fort Myers, where I'd gotten booked to perform at a small club. I was paid $250 for my services. Believe it or not, $250 was all it took to book me at the time. I don't remember much from the club—my shows weren't very memorable back then—but I do know that by the end of the night, I was exhausted. I was drunk, high, sleep-deprived, and all I wanted was to get some rest. But I couldn't bring myself to spend the little bit of paper I'd just made on a motel. Most of my $250 payday was already going toward gas money, since Fort Myers is almost three hours away from Miami, and the club wasn't paying for lodging and transportation. So when we left the club, I tossed my keys to my homie P-Nut and told him to take us back to Miami. I hopped in the passenger seat of my truck and closed my eyes. I figured we'd be back in the crib by the time I woke up.

The problem was I wasn't the only one who was drunk and tired. P-Nut was too. We hadn't been on the road more than twenty minutes when I woke up to the sound and sight of my Cadillac Escalade drifting off the highway. I looked over, and P-Nut was asleep at the wheel. I shouted out, but it was too late. A few seconds (and flips) later, my truck was upside down in the median.

When the police showed up at the scene, they put me in handcuffs and told me I was under arrest. I couldn't believe it. I wasn't the one behind the wheel. It turned out I had an outstanding warrant out of Broward County. I was taken to a local police precinct, where I sat in a holding cell for hours while my homies hustled up some funds for my bail.

Sitting in that cell that night, I felt ready to walk away from music. My head was pounding from the accident. My truck was totaled. I was locked up, and my homies were hitting their mommas for bail money. And for what? So I could drive three hours to perform at a hole-in-the-wall club for $250. Between the wreck and these new criminal charges, this trip to Fort Myers was going to cost me thousands. Money I didn't have. I thought about the crowd at the club hours earlier while I'd performed. Not one person there was fucking with my music. Nobody had come to that club to see me. They were all waiting for me to get off the fucking stage.

The more I thought about my situation, the more my negative thoughts spiraled. This wasn't just a bad night. Things just weren't working out for me in general. I was going on ten years of trying to make it, and I had little to show for all of my pain and struggle. My first deal with Suave House Records had fizzled out. My current deal with Slip-N-Slide Records seemed to be on a similar trajectory. Maybe this hip-hop shit just wasn't going to pan out for me. Maybe I should just get a desk job somewhere. What I didn't know in that moment was that everything I had dreamed of and worked for was on the verge of coming true.

As low as I was that night, I didn't end up throwing in the towel. I picked myself back up and got back to work. A few months later, I heard the beat for what would become "Hustlin'," and the rest is history. My whole life changed.

I share that story to say this. The temptation to fold and wave the white flag is going to be strongest when the finish line is closer than you can see. So when you feel like giving up, take that as a signal to keep going a little bit longer. The reason you can't see the finish line yet is because it's right around the corner. Hard times come with getting money, so if you're going through those hard times, don't stop now. You're only one play away from changing everything.

What I will say about the *when* is this. Don't ever put a deadline on your dreams. I hear people say, "If I don't make it by the time I'm thirty, then I'm just going to give up." To me, that says you really don't want it that bad. Having that mindset is like starting a marathon with a lead weight around your neck. You might as well not even try if you're going into something already thinking about your exit. You can always give up later. Don't start out with that type of negative energy in the back of your mind. If you really love something, then make it your life. In for a penny, in for a pound. Fuck a time limit. Smash that hourglass.

One final thought. I don't wear my wristwatches so that I can tell the time. I've got an iPhone for that. The function of my watch is so that I can walk into a room anywhere in the world and introduce myself to everyone without having to say one word.

CHAPTER

6

REMAIN HANDS-ON

The minute you get too big to mop a floor or wipe a counter, that's the exact minute you have life fucked-up.

—DMX

TWO MONTHS INTO LOCKDOWN AND I WAS still enjoying cutting my grass. The process reminded me how important it is to always remain hands-on, not only when it comes to handling business affairs, but just life in general. Prior to me getting the tractor, I knew very little about the process that went into keeping The Promise Land looking the way I like it to look. I put in a few weeks of yard work, and I had a much better understanding. I knew how long it took for me to do it. I knew how long it would take if I was on the big boy tractor and I had two of my homies riding the shiteaters. I knew how often I needed to gas those things up and how much that costs. And I knew which areas of the estate needed to be manicured at the same level as my beard, and which spots I didn't mind letting the grass grow.

Being hands-on keeps you on top of your shit. If I did hire a lawn service and they quoted me a price for their services, I was going to have an informed opinion of that number. Does this sound fair, or do I need to go get a second opinion because these motherfuckers might be trying to overcharge Rozay and take advantage of me because they think I must not know any better? When you're hands-on, you're more on point, and fewer mistakes get made.

In the rap game, I've seen a lot of talented artists struggle because they weren't actively involved in every aspect of their career. They focused strictly on their art and completely ignored the rest of the business. But success in the music industry depends on a lot more than just the songs you come up with in the studio. You have to be well-rounded. You need to work on marketing yourself and building your fan base. You need to network with other artists and producers. You need to form relationships and politic with the program directors at radio stations and the editors at magazines. If you just leave everything to other people with no questions asked, you're rolling the dice with your career.

Some people are hands-on until they get their first taste of success. Then they stop doing the things that made them successful in the first place. It's not even a decision they're consciously aware of. It's just human nature. Think about it. Once you've had something to eat, you're not going to be as hungry. And if your belly's full, you might not be as inclined to chase down your next meal. That's why it's crucial to always think about the long term. I'm not just trying to secure my next meal. I'm trying to secure every meal for the rest of my children's lives.

Other people get a little bit of clout and let it go to

their head. They gas themselves up. All of a sudden, they're too good to be getting their hands dirty. It usually isn't long before those people are back to where they started.

I was talking to my barber the other day. He's been coming to my crib to cut my hair for years, but prior to the pandemic, he didn't do a lot of house calls outside of me. Now he's doing a lot of them, and he's making a lot more money. His services are in high demand. But even though he's a barber who can now charge $150 a haircut, he's still got to get out of bed when he gets that text at two thirty in the morning from his VIP insomniac client Rozay and make his way over to The Promise Land. He's not above doing that now because he leveled up. Waking up for those 2:30 a.m. haircuts is the real reason he leveled up in the first place.

No matter how much you level up in life, you want to stay connected to what's happening on the ground floor. They say the reason Amazon is so successful is because Jeff Bezos, a man worth damn near $200 billion, still runs his company like it's a start-up. To him, it's always Day 1 at Amazon HQ. Here's what he said in a letter to his shareholders in 2016.

I've been reminding people that it's Day 1 for a couple of decades. I work in an Amazon building named Day 1, and when I moved buildings, I took the name with me. I spend time thinking about this topic. Day 2 is sta-

sis. Followed by irrelevance. Followed by excruciating, painful decline. Followed by death. And that is why it is always Day 1.

I own twenty-five Wingstops, but the first thing I do when I pull up to one is locate the broom and start sweeping. It doesn't matter if I came through in a Rolls-Royce Cullinan. Where's the damn broom at? I do it because having that mindset is what got me to where I'm at. If I want to keep being successful, then I have to keep that same energy. I also do it to lead by example and show my employees that there's no shame in working at a fast-food restaurant when you're starting out. There's no job that's beneath a boss. You can take out the trash and still be a boss. These things are the building blocks. So remember you're never too successful to be hands-on. You're never too rich to hustle hard. And you're most definitely never too big of a boss to cut your own grass.

CHAPTER

7

YOUR CALLING IS NOT
A CONFERENCE CALL

I was nominated, never won a Grammy
But I understand, they'll never understand me

—Rick Ross feat. Drake, "Gold Roses,"
Port of Miami 2 (2019)

I HAD SEVERAL PEOPLE ADVISE ME NOT TO buy The Promise Land. They told me what happened to Holyfield was a cautionary tale about biting off more than you can chew. They said the same thing could happen to me. That my eyes might be bigger than my belly. I took a look in the mirror at my gorgeous physique and I knew there was no possible way that could be true.

This wasn't even coming from nonbelievers who doubted me or enemies who wanted to see my demise. This was coming from close friends and family members. People who genuinely cared about my well-being and truly believed they had my best interests at heart. But despite their best intentions, they didn't understand my vision. Only I did. So I had to ignore their words the same way I would a hater's.

Being that I'm from the 305, I'm a fan of the Miami Heat. Shout-out to Jimmy Buckets, UD, La Spoelstra Nostra and the whole squad. But the Heat Gang member whose career I've followed the longest is the team's president, Pat Riley. "The Godfather" is one of the greatest basketball minds of all time, and every time the OG and I have crossed paths over the years, I've tried to take a peek at his playbook and learn something new. I call his plays "Pat Riley Conspiracies."

During his coaching days, Pat Riley paid close attention to what he called "peripheral opponents," in addition to the teams that were on the schedule. Peripheral opponents were the people and things off the court that got in the way of his players performing at their highest level and staying focused on the team's goal of winning an NBA championship. These distractions came in different shapes and sizes. They were journalists and ESPN talking heads who spoke negatively about the team in the media. They were the team owners and general managers who were engaged in contract disputes with players. They were players' own friends and family members who, in one form or another, were pulling his players' attention away from the game of basketball. It's important to be mindful of the distractions that can come from these peripheral opponents. If you're not vigilant, the voice of a loved one can derail you as much as an enemy's.

In my former life, I used to traffic dope up to Atlanta from Miami. Before I would head home, I would always stop by 794 Evander Holyfield Highway. The heavyweight champ's crib was so big, they named the whole fucking street after him. I'd pull over to the side of the road, smoke a joint and just stare at the house for a while. I told myself then that one day I was going to own it.

When I would look into my future and visualize myself owning the estate, the image in my mind was much bigger than just me living in it. This house was an inspiring symbol of possibility, and I always conceived of it as the headquarters of my empire. A place to make music and films. A place to build brands and partnerships. Somewhere I could invite all different types of like-minded creative people—rappers, singers, producers, musicians, screenwriters and directors—and collaborate on ideas. The Promise Land would be a place where magic happened.

I believe my vision for the estate was much bigger than Holyfield's. But nobody who told me I shouldn't buy the house was going to understand that. How could I expect them to know that this was my destiny? Tell me, who would have believed me if I told them in 2014 that Paramount Pictures and Sony Pictures would pay me millions of dollars to rent my house as a shooting location for major motion pictures? What would my loved ones have said if I tried to explain that in just a few years, Eddie Murphy and Arsenio Hall were going to come to The Promise Land and turn my house into the new royal palace of Zamunda for the sequel to *Coming to America*, my favorite film when I was twelve years old? Or that I would be in the movie, telling General Izzi that King Akeem had just returned from America with a son? Can you imagine how they would have looked at me if I said some shit like that? They would have probably taken Rozay in for a psychiatric evaluation. But lo and behold, *Coming 2 America* is now available to stream on Amazon Prime, and you better believe the biggest boss got that cameo with Wesley Snipes.

Your calling isn't a conference call. It's not a room on Clubhouse that's meant for everyone to voice their opinions and come to a consensus. Your vision is yours alone, and it's not for everyone to understand. If everyone could see what you see, it would be their vision too. If I had listened to all the people who told me my dreams were unattainable, I wouldn't have achieved anything in life.

When you decide to go after something bigger than your current circumstances and go against the grain, there will be doubters. If you don't have any naysayers, you might not be dreaming big enough. They'll tell you your dream is unrealistic, unlikely or outright impossible. Tune all that bullshit out. The people who say those things usually gave up on their dreams a long time ago. When they look at yours, they see what they could never accomplish. Don't ever let external doubt seep into your internal dialogue. You don't need outside approval and validation to go after what you want in life. You've already got the green light to move forward. Hit the gas and go.

CHAPTER

8

YOU ARE YOUR ONLY COMPETITION

Who gives a fuck what a hater's gotta say?
I made a couple million dollars last year dealing weight
—Rick Ross feat. T-Pain, "The Boss," *Trilla* (2008)

MY CLOSE FRIEND DJ KHALED IS ALWAYS talking about "THEY." "STAY AWAY FROM THEY." "THEY DON'T WANT YOU TO WIN." "THEY WANT TO KEEP THE KEYS FROM YOU AND BLOCK YOU FROM THE PATHWAY OF MORE SUCCESS." Khaled is a fucking lunatic. I love my brother to death. I needed to check on my dawg and see how he was holding up during the pandemic.

Who are these people that are sabotaging our success? I used to think I had a lot of enemies. When I was an All-Dade offensive lineman for the Carol City Chiefs, it was my rival opponents at Miami Northwestern. When I hopped off the porch and started getting money in the streets, it was the niggas who tried to short stop the traps where I was hustling. During my ten-year struggle to break into the music industry, I built up a long list of adversaries.

Frustrated with the state of my career, I took out a lot of those frustrations on the industry gatekeepers I'd convinced myself were trying to hold me back. First, I turned on Ted Lucas, who had signed me to Slip-N-Slide Records. Surely he was to blame for my lack of success. So were the radio show hosts at 99 Jamz, like Big Lip Bandit and Supa Cindy, who weren't supporting my music, and the major label A&Rs, like Craig Kallman and Mike Caren at Atlantic Records, who passed on signing me. At one point I even went after Khaled—one of the nicest, most genuine people in this industry—because he wasn't spinning my records at Club Krave on Saturday nights. Can you believe I used to think Khaled was a "They"?

I stepped to Trick Daddy for claiming he was the "Mayor of Miami." I sent shots at T.I. for saying he was the "King of the South." I first picked a fight with 50 Cent, a feud that's lasted more than a decade, because I didn't like the way he looked at me at the 2008 BET Hip-Hop Awards.

I've never been one to shy away from competition or confrontation. Having an opponent to go head-to-head with excites me. If I'm being honest, I probably enjoy going to war a little too much. Once somebody's name makes it onto my shitlist there's no lengths I won't go to humiliate them and make them appear minuscule. If I was an NBA player, I'd be the motherfucker throwing down 360 tomahawk jams when there's two minutes left in the game and I'm already up by 20. I can't tell you why I'm like this. My DNA might be a little different from most niggas.

Unfortunately, going to war very rarely results in success. When my career did take off, it had absolutely nothing to do with me dissing Ted or putting a bounty on Khaled's Terror Squad chain. If anything, those things did me a disservice and actually held me back. I was burning bridges and focusing on other motherfuckers. My success would come from one thing: me making incredible music.

I love beefing with niggas. But I've come to learn there's very little to gain from it. If there was, believe me, I would do it every day. Diss records are rarely hit records, and as much as I enjoy squashing a fuck boy, it's not worth the negative energy and drama it brings. People have told me I ended my enemies' careers, and as much as I enjoy hearing that and would love to take credit for their demise, I know that's not really true. If they could make another hit record, they would have a career.

The biggest threat to your success will never be another motherfucker. If you think someone else is the problem, you really have very little control over your situation. You can't change other people. If you realize you're the one holding yourself back, you can do something about that.

The things that have posed the biggest threats to my success have been things I had to address within myself. The closest I've come to losing everything I worked for was when I started having seizures due to lack of sleep, among other bad habits. The second closest time was when I caught a case. To overcome those situations, I had to battle my own demons and confront the enemy within. I had to compete with myself and win those battles. I had to get more rest. I had to start exercising and eating better. I had to stop putting myself in risky situations. Those were the wars I really needed to win.

Spite can be a powerful motivator, but it can also impact your judgment. Motherfuckers will try to draw you into shit, but you have to resist the urge to take the bait. You have to know when to let shit go. Those words of wisdom were passed down to me from Kenneth "Boobie" Williams, one of the infamous dope boys I came up around in Carol City in the late eighties and early nineties. Boobie was a prolific hustler who built a criminal empire that came to be worth more than $80 million. But at the time he shared those words with me, Boobie's days were numbered. My dawg was on *America's Most Wanted*, but it wasn't all the dope he was selling that put the feds' target on his back. It was all the bodies dropping. Boobie had gotten caught up in going to war with enemies, and it had brought down his whole empire. It was too late for his words to save him, but it wasn't too late for me. You have to know when to give a pass.

I've moved beyond beefing with niggas. The only person I'm competing with now is the lesser version of myself. At this point in my life, I'm trying to make power plays and partner with Fortune 500 companies. If you're like me and having an axe to grind or a chip on your shoulder brings out the best in you, then use those things to light a fire inside you and outwork everyone else. Don't let those feelings control you and distract you from what's really important.

Success is the best revenge, and success comes from creation and collaboration, not conflict and destruction. So keep your eyes on the prize and stick to the script. Stay focused on achieving your objectives, working on yourself and moving closer toward your goals.

With that being said, I want to take this opportunity to extend an olive branch to any of my remaining enemies. I'm willing to wipe the slate clean and start anew. See how much I've matured? I just need one favor from you in return. I need you to take a photo of yourself standing in front of one of my Wingstop locations holding up a bottle of Luc Belaire and post it to your IG. Not on your story. It needs to be a proper post on the grid. And I need you to hold the bottle up at eye level, give or take an inch.

I'm giving you one year to post it. After that, the offer's off the table and I can't promise that I won't revert into the old me. Remember, I'm the same motherfucker who named his album *God Forgives, I Don't*. This is a once-in-a-lifetime opportunity and I highly suggest that you take advantage of it. You should probably start planning your photo shoot now. Oh, and one last thing. It needs to be one of the electrolumines-

CHAPTER

9

FAILURE IS PART OF THE PROCESS

I'M NOT SUCCESSFUL BECAUSE I WOKE UP one morning in the fall of 2005 and decided to make an iconic anthem called "Hustlin'" that everybody and their momma would love. Believe it or not, my success has very little to do with the day I recorded "Hustlin'." The reason I'm successful is that for ten years before "Hustlin'," I woke up every day and made music that nobody gave a fuck about. I signed deals that went nowhere. I dropped mixtapes that people wouldn't accept for free. I released singles that made no impact at radio. And I kept going anyway. That's why I'm successful.

I've continued to be successful in the fifteen years since "Hustlin'" because I've kept the same energy and continued to weather every storm that came my way. Success is not a straight line. It's not a linear process. It's a long journey with many ups and downs and twists and turns. It's not like I got my major label deal and it's been smooth sailing ever since.

In the ten years after "Hustlin'," I had to overcome just as many setbacks as I did in the ten years prior. It was a different type of struggle. I was most definitely much more famous and financially secure. But like the late, great Notorious B.I.G. once said, "Mo Money Mo Problems." I had to deal with bloggers assassinating my character and trying to take away everything I'd worked for. I survived multiple attempts on my life. I suffered health scares that were so bad, they had me in the ICU on life support. I caught a case where I was facing life. But no matter how many times I stumbled, I never gave up. Every time I picked myself back up, dusted my shirt off and got back to being the boss. That's why I'm successful.

Failure is not the dream killer with the biggest body count. It's the fear of failure that prevents most people from realizing their dreams and living up to their full potential. Most people never win because they're so afraid of losing. They know what they want but can't bring themselves to fully commit because what if it goes wrong? They give up on their goals because they're afraid of rejection. Or they give it a go one time and then give up at the first sign of difficulty. They choose to play it safe and stay in their comfort zone. But your comfort zone is where your goals go to die.

Ten albums in, journalists have started to ask me to rank my discography in interviews. That's always a tough one. That's like someone asking you to rank your children. All of my albums represent different stages of my life, and depending on how I'm feeling on that particular day, my rankings could be totally different than the last time I got asked that question. But my number one on the list usually remains the same: *Deeper than Rap.*

It's not that I think my raps or the beats on *Deeper than Rap* are better than the others. That's not the case at all. The reason *Deeper than Rap* is my favorite album is because, more than any other, my back was against the wall when I made it. I recorded *Port of Miami* following the success of "Hustlin'" when I was on a rocket ship headed to the top. I released *God Forgives, I Don't* at the peak of my powers. I felt like an emperor looking down on his subjects. I was facing life in prison when I recorded *Black Market,* so I had my back against the wall again in that sense, but the people were still on my side and wanted to see me win. *Deeper than Rap* is special to me because I made it at a time when I'd lost all my momentum from '06 to '08 and it seemed like everyone was counting me out. This was around the time of the whole correctional officer controversy and my beef with 50 Cent. For years, 50 had been the biggest bully in the rap game, and a lot of motherfuckers thought he was going to take me out for good. The odds were stacked against me heading into the release of *Deeper than Rap,* but I beat those odds. I came out on top.

It's hard to put into words how powerful that made me feel and how much strength it gave me moving forward. Every setback or failure I experienced from that point on felt manageable. I felt bulletproof. That feeling was what led to me naming my next album *Teflon Don*. Because I knew I had it in me to survive any shots that came my way. I already had. I'm successful because I'm not afraid to fail. And I'm not afraid to fail because I've already failed countless times and come back stronger every time. What you get by facing your fear of failure is not as important as who you become. The more you face your fears, the higher tolerance you have for what feels scary. It's mental weight training.

Growth requires risk. When I think about the major breakthroughs in my own life, they all required me to face discomfort and take a leap of faith. I know it's not easy to take risks. That's why most people tend to stick to what's familiar, because it feels safer. When you strive for something that seems outside your reach, you risk discomfort, humiliation and failure. But there's no reward without risk. At the end of the day, you have to be willing to step outside your comfort zone. If you're not willing to put down a big bet on yourself, you can close this book now, take your seat in the bleachers and watch other niggas compete for glory. Because I don't know of too many people who achieved greatness by playing everything safe.

Fear is natural. Let me take that one step further. Fear is good. It's an indication that you're onto something. Fear tells you what you need to do. The more you fear something, the more you care about it, which means the more important it is that you conquer it. It's okay to be scared, but it's not okay to let your fears paralyze you. Taking no action is much more dangerous than taking the wrong action.

All the pioneers and trailblazers we look up to felt fear and took losses. But they didn't conquer their fears by waiting around, hoping for them to miraculously disappear. Confidence doesn't work that way. You build confidence by embracing uncertainty and the possibility that you'll embarrass yourself. By being so scared that you might shit yourself and then still deciding to go for it anyway. That's what having courage is. You don't need to be fearless or flawless so long as you're persistent.

What a lot of motherfuckers don't seem to understand is that failure is a part of the process of success. We learn by making mistakes.

So what if you do fail? Fuck it. The most dangerous motherfucker in the world is the one who can lose it all and then get it back. So as long as you're still breathing, you better get up and give it another go. All the real hustlers fell and bumped their heads at one point or another. Did they curl up in a ball and die afterward? Nah. They got back up and dusted themselves off. Then they got back on the horse of life and got that bitch to trot. Before long they were in full stride.

CHAPTER

10

TEAMWORK MAKES THE DREAM WORK

I taught all my niggas how to fish. Some caught more than others. Some said they'd rather be fed. Some passed me up in the process. But at the end of it all I know I ain't hide the game from my people and I'm real for that.

—Nipsey Hussle (2017)

AS MUCH FUN AS I WAS HAVING CUTTING my grass, I knew I wouldn't be out on my tractor every week forever. Once the lockdown got lifted and things started to get back to normal, that would no longer be the best use of my time. As much as I strive to be hands-on and maintain a baseline level of involvement in all of my affairs, I can't do it all. I'm an artist and entertainer before anything else. I need to be able to focus on what I do best and delegate other tasks to people that I trust.

I'm blessed to have an incredible team that's behind me. I wouldn't be where I'm at without them. I have my momma, Ella, and my sister, Renee, my most trusted confidants, who have a hand in everything that I do. I have Yvette, MMG's general manager, who connects all the dots in the music industry. I have Lex running point on promotions, marketing and branding. I have my DJ Sam Sneak. I have Slab by my side every time I hit the stage to help hype up the crowd. I have my road manager Geter K, who makes sure everything runs smoothly when I'm out of town. I have my security, Jerry and Ducky, who keep the fuck boys from around me. I've got Skinny and Tom holding shit down at the Atlanta estate and Kano and Short Legs in Miami. I have my criminal defense attorney, Steve Sadow, and my entertainment lawyer, Leron.

I may be the head of this empire, but all these people make up the backbone. A backbone consists of many vertebrae, and if just one of them is out of alignment, the whole body suffers. That means that the people you choose to surround yourself with is not a decision to take lightly. Your network affects your net worth. It's hard to make the right moves if you're running with the wrong people.

Whenever you hear stories about an athlete or entertainer going broke, you usually hear about how many people they were taking care of. How they had become an ATM machine for all their friends and family members until one day the money faucet stopped dripping and it all came crashing down. That could never happen to me because I don't associate with bloodsucking leeches. The people who I surround myself with aren't around to ride their successful friend's coattails. I like to think I've blessed my people with opportunities to improve their lives, but I've never been someone's meal ticket. All of the people you see around me are bringing something to the table. So it's my responsibility to make sure everybody eats.

I'm not saying I don't hire or invest in my close friends and family members. Most of those names I just mentioned are my day ones. I believe the loyalty that you find in people who were down when you had nothing is hard to replicate. If someone is going to have a hand in your success, you want it to be someone who gives a fuck about you. When people who don't genuinely care about you are responsible for making decisions that impact you, those decisions are usually going to be in their best interests, not yours.

But it's one thing to be friends and family, and it's another thing when business is involved. So if I put someone on the payroll, that means we're on the same page when it comes to getting money. I have a few lazy motherfuckers in my life who I love from the bottom of my heart, but there are zero lazy motherfuckers in my life who I subsidize. I would be doing them a disservice if I did that. A true friend is someone who pushes you and encourages you to become the best version of yourself. They don't enable your bad habits and tendencies.

When you find like-minded people who are loyal and on the same page as you, those are the people you want to keep close and build with. That's your power circle. Don't take these people for granted because that never ends well. That's the quickest way to plant seeds of disloyalty and insubordination in your crew, and that shit will spread like cancer. If you only try to extract value from your people without giving it back, eventually that's going to come back to haunt you. Those people will only be around for as long as they need you, and when the tables turn and the day comes when you need them more than they need you, they're going to be nowhere to be found.

You have to empower your people. As soon as I got in the game, I reached back and pulled Gunplay, Torch and Young Breed up to the big leagues with me and introduced the world to Triple C's. I didn't even have my own imprint deal with Def Jam, but I told them if they wanted to put out another Rick Ross album, they were going to have to put out a Triple C's album first. The homies I'd come up with had stuck it out with me through all the trials and tribulations when they could have jumped ship. I had to reward their loyalty and give them an opportunity to win with me.

I've seen niggas get to a position of power and forget to put their team on. It's as if they fall in love with being the one in the spotlight and don't want to share it with anyone. They want to be the top dog and they don't want anyone underneath them to outgrow their positions. But I'm not interested in stacking up my own private collection of victories and hoarding them for myself. I couldn't consider myself to be successful if I wasn't helping other people succeed too.

I don't hold my people back. I don't hire my homies for jobs they can grow into. I hire them for jobs they can one day grow out of. At times, that can be bitter-sweet when it means having to let someone go off and do their own thing, but just because something is sad or hard to do doesn't mean it's a bad thing. It's really a blessing when that happens. If you truly love someone, you want to see them boss up whether it's with you or on their own.

Take Meek Mill and Wale, for example. You don't see them next to me all the time like you did ten years ago. That's by design. Meek and Wale are bosses now too. There was a time when their rank was soldiers under the general and they played that position well until they graduated from that rank. They're still MMG and we're always going to be partners and get money together. But there came a point when I recognized it was time for them to focus on building their own empires. That was the plan all along. When Meek started pushing his Dream Chasers imprint, I went and got the logo tatted on my fucking face. He repped my shit for so long and helped me build my empire, I couldn't wait to do the same for him. I felt the same way about Wale's Every Blue Moon. I apply that same principle to all my homies' ventures. I champion them like they're mine. I've always looked at it like we're all in this shit together.

Going back to what I was saying earlier, for argument's sake, let's imagine a scenario where one day I go broke. Ha! HA! Okay, now that I've gotten that out of my system, let me regain my composure and try that one more time. Let's say they bring back prohibition and I'm no longer allowed to sell Luc Belaire. Or the whole world goes vegan and so I have to close my Wingstops because eating chicken is considered animal cruelty. Better yet, let's say I suffer a seizure or a stroke that leaves me so fucked-up, I'm left with an alligator arm and I can't even hold up a microphone to rap ever again. What do you think happens to all the people around me? Do you think everybody goes broke because their money faucet got turned off? Guess again. All of my people have gotten themselves to a place where they're in a position to help me get back on my feet if I should fall.

My momma and sister handle a lot of my business affairs, but these days they also have investments that are completely independent of me. My momma owns more than a dozen rental properties. My sister has a car dealership. If you're in the Olive Branch, Mississippi, area and looking to get a new car, go hit up B&J Auto Sales and ask for Tawanda Roberts. Don't even worry if your credit is not the best. Everybody gets approved at B&J Auto.

At this point, I don't even know about half the shit my people are involved in. I'm trying to tell you, I gave them an opportunity and then they all went out and got fucking rich. I swear to God I can't remember the last time anyone in my inner circle asked me for a handout. It's been years. That's what happens when you pick the right team and empower your people.

CHAPTER

11

STACK YOUR PAPER

THE GOVERNMENT WAS CUTTING EVERY-body $1,200 stimulus checks. Millions of Americans had lost their jobs due to the pandemic, and the way things were looking, they weren't going to be getting back to work anytime soon. But $1,200 didn't seem like very much. You can only stretch a stack so far. So what was going to happen once those stimmy checks dried up? Unless they had some more savings stashed away, pretty soon a lot of people were going to be jammed up.

I can see how, from the outside looking in, it might appear that I've been irresponsible with my earnings. I do have a 235-acre estate. I do have a 350,000-gallon swimming pool. I do have a lot of cars. I do buy jewelry. I do own three horses. I have all the extravagant rapper shit and then some. Guilty as charged.

But remember, I bought The Promise Land at a heavy discount. Then I turned it into an asset and monetized it. In 2017, Sony Pictures cut a nice check to film *Superfly* here. That movie had a $30 million budget. Two years later, Paramount Pictures used the estate as the primary shooting location for *Coming 2*

America. That had a $60 million budget. I've had a lot more movie producers come by because they were considering using it. Even when they don't decide to use it, they still have to pay me just to visit. I rent my cars out too. The Promise Land is an asset that generates income, not a liability that drains my finances. The place is already paying for itself.

I do enjoy luxuries, but my assets far outweigh my liabilities. I've never bought something that I couldn't afford to buy twice. I don't live beyond my means. I might be a big spender, but I've always been a much bigger saver.

When I signed my major label deal with Def Jam, I received a seven-figure advance. After a decade of struggle, I'd be lying if I said I wasn't tempted to finally reward myself for all my years of struggle and unpaid labor. As big as that advance was, I could have very quickly blown through that million. For years I had dreamed of all the things I would have once I made it, and now there was nothing stopping me from going out and acquiring those things. But I didn't. For the next nine months, I pretended that money didn't exist. I put my head down and got back to work. I was in high demand, so I hit the road and gave the people what they wanted. I performed "Hustlin'" for every venue that had a bag for the boss. I saved that money too. The deposits and the back ends. It wasn't until *Port of Miami* debuted at number one that I felt comfortable making my first big purchase. I bought my studio house in Atlanta, which I still own to this day.

Coming up in Miami, I saw a lot of hustlers—I'm talking about in the streets and in the rap game—get fast money and lose it even faster. Miami is a city where motherfuckers like to show out. It's not a place where people are quiet about getting money. In New England, you might pull up to a red light and have no idea that the guy in the Prius next to you is sitting on $100 million. Miami is not like that. Here people exaggerate how much money they actually have. Most of those Lamborghinis you see on South Beach are rented.

Uncle Luke was the founding father of hip-hop in Miami, and I saw with my own eyes how quickly he went from dropping double-platinum albums to being forced to declare bankruptcy and sell off his entire catalog. My worst nightmare was that something similar could happen to me. I knew my major label deal didn't guarantee me major success. Def Jam's roster was full of artists they'd signed and since forgotten about.

I hadn't come into the game with a loyal underground fan base that had been supporting my music for years and would continue to support me if this deal with Def Jam didn't work out. All of my success to date was based entirely on one hit record. That indicated to me that it was too soon for me to start celebrating and spending money. That advance was my only safety net in the world.

Seeing the pandemic play out was a harsh reminder of how important it is to have a rainy-day fund. I know most people aren't in the position I'm in to keep duffel bags of unmarked bills and gold bullion buried in discrete locations across the Southeastern United States. Most people live check to check. Regardless, I think everyone has something they spend their money on that they know they could live without. I already told you about a few of my vices. What are yours?

The difference is I've gotten myself to a point where I can afford to have luxuries. Until you can, I encourage you to figure out what you can sacrifice to start building some savings. I can't tell you when your rainy-day fund is going to come in handy, but I can guarantee you that that day will come. Why do you think I titled my first memoir *Hurricanes*? Storms are a major part of life. The only thing that you can control is how prepared you are to handle them when they hit. When it rains, it pours, and when it does, nobody is coming with an umbrella to keep you dry. You're going to be on your own. So you'll be grateful if you tucked your last tax refund instead of throwing it in the air at Magic City.

When you make the decision to prioritize saving and investing your money over spending, you make a trade-off. You're choosing to sacrifice immediate gratification in exchange for the possibility of an even better outcome in the future. It's not a hard concept to wrap your head around, but when you're from a conflict- and crime-ridden area, making that calculation is a little more complicated. Think about it. If you're living in a world where there's a real significant chance you can lose your life, you're going to be less inclined to sacrifice the present to invest in a future that isn't guaranteed. You're also probably going to be more likely to engage in self-destructive behavior—cheating, lying, stealing—because you're not considering the devastating long-term consequences of that shit. If that mindset applies to you, you're going to have to rewire your thinking and start playing the long game.

Once you've built up your rainy-day fund in case of emergencies, you can start acquiring assets that earn passive income. Bosses don't just work for money. They put their money to work. Whether it's through buying stocks, bonds or real estate, you want to work toward establishing passive streams of income. Assets are a key part of accumulating wealth. Work leads to money. Money leads to assets. Assets lead to wealth.

Good financial habits build wealth and bad ones destroy it. If you spend everything you earn, an increase in money will just result in an increase in spending and you'll never be able to build wealth.

The best thing that money will ever buy you is some peace of mind. When you get to a certain level of money, it takes the pressure off and frees you up to focus on the things you really care about. Financial

CHAPTER

12

WAR READY

MY MILITARY-GRADE HUMVEE FINALLY arrived. As the highly decorated five-star general of the Maybach Music Group, I felt it was only right I get one. It was perfect. Well, it was almost perfect. There were still a few modifications I wanted to make. I was planning to take out the black seats and replace them with custom ones made from Louis Vuitton leather. I felt the brown monogrammed canvas would contrast with the green camouflage exterior paint job beautifully. Shout-out to my homie Tee over at Exclusive Game for making that happen. I was also looking into the legality of strapping a .50-caliber Gatling gun to the roof.

I hired two new members to my estate's security team: K9 Doc and K9 Midas, two highly trained Belgian Malinois guard dogs. During the extensive interview process, Doc and Midas told me personally how much they despise trespassers. My prayers go out to the next lost soul who thinks they can just stroll into The Promise Land without a proper invitation.

I hadn't beefed up security at the estate in response to an incident. I did it in anticipation of future unforeseen circumstances. Times of peace are when you prepare for battle. If you wait until you're under siege to see what's in your war chest, you're going to get slaughtered. You need to premeditate as many moves as you can for all potential scenarios. You need to remain war ready.

Think chess, not checkers. The only time you should be thinking Checkers is when you're hungry. In that case, I suggest you make your way over to my fine dining establishment located at the corner of 183rd Street and 27th Avenue in Carol City. Order yourself a Big Buford, a chili dog and a blue slush. Tell them Rozay sent you. Once you've had something to eat, get back to plotting your moves on your chessboard.

A chess master is never caught off guard. Whatever move their opponent makes, they already have a counterattack ready to go. They don't even have to think about it because they already had a plan in place for what they would do in the event that happened. They've prepared for every possible scenario so they don't start panicking when one of their pawns gets picked off. They're ready to take some losses and make adjustments as they advance across the board. They know that losses come with the game, and so they stick to the plan, strategically backing their opponent into a corner until there's nowhere left for them to go. At that point, it's game over. Checkmate. Then you reset the board and prepare for the next game.

Being war ready isn't just about having a contingency plan in place for when shit hits the fan. It's deeper than buying tanks and guard dogs. What I'm really trying to stress to you is the importance of preparation. Because it's not just the storms you need to prepare for. You have to be ready for life's blessings too. A once-in-a-lifetime opportunity that suddenly presents itself is worthless if you're not in the right position to capitalize on it. I was talking about having a rainy-day fund in case of emergencies, but ideally you also want to have some funds stashed away for when a life-changing investment opportunity comes your way. The importance of planning and preparation goes both ways, and if you're not prepared, you better believe someone else will be. Your loss will be their gain.

In his fifth book, *Mastery*, Robert Greene writes that "a fighter who enters the ring with a clear sense of purpose and strategy, and with the confidence that comes from complete preparation, has a much better chance of prevailing." I was reminded of those words during a recent visit from one of my good homies, four-time world champion boxer Adrien "About Billions" Broner.

When it comes to talent and ability, there's not a lot of motherfuckers who can step in the ring and outbox AB. But when AB came by the house, he told how he was in the process of getting his career back on track after digging himself into a deep hole. My homie fell off the pound-for-pound rankings in recent years after losing important fights he should have won. He'll be the first to admit those losses were due to lack of preparation and focus. He'd let himself get heavy between fights, and then when it was time to get ready for the next one, he had to put all his energy toward making weight at the last minute when he should have been studying tape on his opponent and sharpening his skills. He's paid a steep price for that lack of preparation. It altered the course of his career. It felt good to see my dawg. He finally seemed focused, and I truly believe his best performances are still to come. I'm not saying any of this to speak down on my brother. I'm just saying that there are consequences to not being war ready.

The best fighters don't let themselves get fat in between fights. They stay in elite shape year-round. Up-and-coming contenders never know when Floyd Mayweather's or Conor McGregor's scheduled opponent is going to get injured and the promoters are going to be looking for a last-minute replacement fighter. Getting a chance to prove yourself against the best of your generation would be the opportunity of a lifetime for any prizefighter. But if they're not prepared to step on the scale and make weight, then it's just a wasted opportunity.

Two weeks after my Humvee got delivered, a forty-six-year-old Black man was killed in Minneapolis, Minnesota. His name was George Floyd. He died at the hands of the Minneapolis Police Department, after a white police officer named Derek Chauvin put his knee on his neck for eight minutes and forty-six seconds. His fellow officers stood by and did nothing as brother George ran out of oxygen, begging for his life and calling out for his momma. They did nothing when he told them he couldn't breathe. That's how he died.

Learning about George Floyd's life hurt my heart. He and I were around the same age, and like me, George had gone to college on a football scholarship and dropped out to pursue a passion for music. In the nineties, he'd been down with DJ Screw and the Screwed Up Click in Houston.

I was angry and I was disgusted, but I wasn't surprised. As upsetting as that video was, I wasn't shocked in the least bit. I was four years old when five white Miami-Dade police officers beat Arthur McDuffie to death in Liberty City. I was seven when they killed Nevell Johnson in Overtown. I was thirteen when they killed Clement Lloyd and Allan Blanchard in Overtown. I was sixteen when they beat down Rodney King in Los Angeles. I was thirty-eight when Darren Wilson killed Michael Brown in Ferguson.

I got the keys to the city, still we left in the cold
Hands in the sky, still was left in the road
Ribbon in the sky, Michael Brown, another soul

Stole by the system, Black men we pay the toll

The price is your life, Uncle Sam want a slice

Black dress code now we looting in the night

Now we throwing Molotovs in this holocaust

And I know they hate to hear me screaming, "I'm a boss"

—Rick Ross, "Don't Shoot" (2014)

I was thirty-eight when they killed Tamir Rice in Cleveland. I was thirty-nine when they killed Freddie Gray in Baltimore. And I was forty-four when they killed George Floyd in Minneapolis. So I wasn't surprised by what happened to George Floyd or that people took to the streets and started burning shit. How can anyone expect people who have been targeted and persecuted for so long to not eventually explode?

I had plans to go down to Miami for a rally the following week and march alongside Trayvon Martin's father in Miramar. But when I saw what was happening twenty minutes away from The Promise Land, I felt compelled to take action. Protestors were clashing with police downtown, and they were getting hit with tear gas, batons and rubber bullets. The governor had declared a state of emergency in Fulton County and dispatched five hundred National Guard members to assist local law enforcement. If the crackers were coming in their Humvees to help the police, then I was coming in mine on behalf of the people.

They say we just a bunch of thugs, don't stand for nothin'
Disgrace to our race, don't belong in public
It was us against the world from the first day
Let us bow our heads, may we all pray
Throwing bricks at the man, we gon' make it
Genocide not in the plans, we gon' make it
Pray my son understand, we gon' make it
Know God holding our hands, we gon' make it
    —Rick Ross, "We Gon Make It," *Black Dollar* (2015)

As I rode through the streets of downtown Atlanta, I couldn't help but think this time felt different. Even though I'd seen this movie many times, for some reason the stakes felt higher. Like just maybe it could actually lead to something. Maybe it was because of the pandemic. People were already at a tipping point, and George Floyd's murder had sent them over the edge. These were dark times we were living in. It seemed like we might be on the verge of a second civil war. I prayed for peace, but I was prepared for war. Either way, I'd be ready.

CHAPTER

13

YOUR HUSTLE DETERMINES YOUR SALARY

Ambition is priceless, that's something that's in your veins
And I doubt that ever change

—Wale feat. Rick Ross and Meek Mill, "Ambition,"
Ambition (2011)

RIDING AROUND IN MY NEW HUMVEE HAD me feeling like Master P when he brought the gold tank out on the basketball court for the "Make 'Em Say Uhh!" music video. That was the one where he had the gorilla mascot doing acrobatic dunks and Shaquille O'Neal made a cameo. That whole No Limit era was so legendary.

"Make 'Em Say Uhh!" was the record that took Master P and No Limit Records out of the Calliope Projects of New Orleans and introduced them to the mainstream in 1998. I was twenty-two years old, and I was heavy in the streets at the time. I'd graduated from my neighborhood and started taking trips out of town, where there was a lot less competition and a lot more money to be made. My dream to make it as a rapper wasn't paying the bills yet. It wasn't even bringing in a penny. So I was ten toes deep in the dope game.

But that year was a major turning point in my life. As Master P's master plan was coming together, my world was closing in on me. Federal indictments started coming down, and it seemed like damn near everybody I knew and looked up to growing up was getting locked up and sent away for decades. Those events were what really shook me and prompted me to go all in on music.

Like me, Master P had early dreams of playing ball in the big leagues. He'd gone to college on a basketball scholarship but dropped out his freshman year to pursue a different path as an entertainer and entrepreneur. It wasn't a seamless transition. For a while he had one foot in and one foot out of the streets like I did. It wasn't until his brother was murdered in 1990 that he decided to wash his hands of the street life.

I could identify with Master P's story. So when "Make 'Em Say Uhh!" blew up and No Limit took over the rap game, Master P was the living, breathing embodiment of a young nigga from the South who got it out the mud. You had to respect his hustle.

I was taking a trip down memory lane the other day, and I came across my first-ever on-camera interview. It was at Poe Boy Studios in Miami. You can pull it up on YouTube. This was back in the early 2000s. I didn't even have a beard yet. At the time, I was a disgruntled artist signed to Slip-N-Slide Records, and I wanted to get off the label and go independent. I talked a lot of shit in that interview, but I also tipped my hat to P for giving me the blueprint on how to build an independent empire.

Thinking of a master plan,
Now I could put a hundred grand in the palm of a
    nigga's hands

I need to hit a lick drastically
I ain't talking Slip-N-Slide but Master P

—Rick Ross, "2003 Freestyle"

I could find a way to credit Master P's influence on
me in every chapter of this book if I wanted. The way
he negotiated his deals and advocated for taking less
money up front in exchange for retaining ownership
and independence over big cash advances from major
labels. The way he built his brand through street-level
guerilla marketing and the iconic gold tank. The way
he put his people on and made No Limit a true family-
owned-and-operated Black business. All of his different ventures outside of music. No Limit Clothing. No
Limit Films. No Limit Sports Management. You can
find a Master P version of every aspect of my success.

Getting money only time for me I ever be at peace
I'mma build a mansion, sit it on Virginia Key
I'm the only one who did it big as Master P
Talking nine figures rapping on these niggas' beats

—Rick Ross, "Richer Than I Ever Been,"
Richer Than I Ever Been (2021)

So it was a no-brainer when an opportunity to part-
ner up with Master P and James "Fly" Lindsay on Rap
Snacks came across my plate. Not only had I admired
Master P for decades, but I also knew James, who has

worked closely with Meek Mill for years, and I held him in high regard. James founded Rap Snacks all the way back in 1994, but it wasn't until recently that the company really started to take off and establish itself as a force to be reckoned with in the snack foods category. That's a testament to James's character. You've got to be a true hustler to be willing to wait twenty-five years to see your plans come to fruition.

I had a lot of respect for Rap Snacks because it was a company born out of hip-hop culture. This wasn't some huge multinational snacks corporation that was trying to use hip-hop to make themselves some money. This was a Black-owned business I wanted to support and see win whether or not I was getting money with them.

The company had seen a lot of success with its product launches with Migos, Cardi B, Boosie, Fabolous and Lil Yachty. Now James and Master P were gearing up to take Rap Snacks to the next level by expanding their distribution network and extending their product line beyond potato chips into ramen noodles and beverages. I wanted in on that expansion. James and I chopped it up and started brainstorming about different products and flavor profiles that aligned with my brand and complemented their roster. A few months later, we made it official, and now my Sweet Chili Lemon Pepper potato chips and Lobster Bisque–flavored ramen noodles are available in over 4,200 Walmart stores nationwide.

Am I really just a narcissist
'Cause I wake up to a bowl of lobster bisque?

—Rick Ross, "I Love My Bitches,"
God Forgives, I Don't (2012)

At the root of all of Master P's moves, and all of mine, was the same thing: ambition. As much as Master P—or any of my influences—may have inspired me and shared the game, he didn't give me the burning desire that pushed me every day and kept me going when I had every reason in the world to give up. That came from within. Ambition isn't something another person can give you.

Wale's and Meek Mill's successes are my proudest achievements as the CEO of Maybach Music Group. We've made a lot of money and classic records together over the last ten years, but my true profit has been getting to watch them live out their dreams. I remember when I first signed them like it was yesterday. Wale was a year removed from getting dropped from Interscope Records. Meek was just starting to get a buzz back going after a prison bid had cost him his first record deal with T.I. Neither of them had much when we first met. Just their dreams. Now they're both multimillionaires. Getting to be a part of their journeys is more rewarding than any points I had on their albums.

I have to admit, I got lucky with those two. The reason I say I got lucky is because when I made the decision to sign them to MMG, I did it for the wrong reasons. I signed them purely based on their talent and potential. I had just launched my label imprint at Warner Bros., and I still had a lot to learn as a record label executive. Talent and potential were all I thought I was supposed to be looking for back then. I didn't even think to evaluate them based on their character. I just assumed that every artist wanted to make it as bad as I did and was willing to do whatever it took. I was wrong when I made that general assumption, but lucky for me, Wale and Meek did want it that bad.

Not every artist I signed had that same ambition. I can't lie, that took a toll on my spirit. It's part of the reason why I've taken a break from signing new artists in recent years. Those types of disappointments are frustrating, especially when you feel a certain sense of responsibility for someone else's success. When I sign an artist, I make a debt to them that I'm going to work harder for them than anyone else they could have signed to. So it's frustrating and discouraging when you get the feeling that you want to see someone win more than they want it for themselves. A team can't win a championship if the coach wants to win more than the players do.

There are plenty of artists who have sold more re-cords than I have. I have one platinum album and it took ten years to move a million copies of that. Plenty of artists can charge more for a verse than I can. I don't draw the biggest crowds or have the most followers on social media. So how is it that when it comes to get-ting money, very few of my peers have accumulated my level of wealth? How's that possible? The answer is simple. I wanted it more than them. So I outworked all these niggas.

Name a motherfucker who hustled harder than Rozay. I've been on the road picking up back ends every weekend for fifteen years straight. Aside from this pandemic, the only break I ever took was when I started having seizures, and I only did that because my momma begged me to. If she hadn't, I would have kept going. I wouldn't give a fuck if I had a seizure on stage and started doing the electric slide. But you gotta pay me extra if you want to see that.

Triple beam dreams, the ghetto is my reality
I'm from where your hustle determines your salary

> —Rick Ross feat. Nas, "Triple Beam Dreams,"
> *Rich Forever* (2012)

Thomas Edison, the greatest inventor in American history, once said, "Genius is one percent inspiration and ninety-nine percent perspiration." That means that when it comes to being successful, your ambition and your work ethic are much more important assets than any God-given talent you're blessed with. That's coming from Ricky Rozay, one of the most talented motherfuckers you've ever seen in your life.

I hope this book will inspire someone to get up off their ass and work toward their goals, but it's not going to do the work for them. You have to have ambition. The dream is free, but the hustle is sold separately. And your hustle is what ultimately determines your salary.

CHAPTER

14

MANAGE THE EMOTIONS

Crib bigger than a church, Lord know I'm blessed
Five different lawyers, Lord know I'm stressed
A punch in the face get you 300K
Ask Vlad, now he's back to making minimum wage

—Rick Ross feat. CeeLo, "Tears of Joy,"
Teflon Don (2010)

EVERY TIME I PERFORM, MY GOAL IS TO GIVE my fans a show that they'll remember for the rest of their lives. When I'm in album mode, my work isn't finished until I know I've made the best music that I'm capable of making. I don't give a fuck how many times the label calls begging me to turn it in. When I get behind a brand like Wingstop or Luc Belaire, I care about how many wings and bottles they sell as much as my album sales. I'm a passionate motherfucker. I take all this shit personally.

I'm emotionally invested in everything I do. But I don't allow my emotions to dictate my decisions. That hasn't always been the case. One area of my life where I've experienced growth is how I handle stressful situations. I used to be a much more reactive person. I've slapped a lot of motherfuckers over minor infractions. Before they even knew they'd offended me, their glasses went flying off their faces.

Coming up in Carol City, you had to be that way. Reactions are survival-oriented, and in the streets, the ability to react quickly to a dangerous situation could mean the difference between life and death. But my life today is much different than it was back in the day, and as I've gotten older, the instincts that once served me started doing me a disservice.

Halfway into 2008, my rap career was on an upward trajectory. My second album, *Trilla*, debuted at number one on the *Billboard* 200, beating the curse of the sophomore slump and silencing any remaining haters who claimed I'd be a one-hit wonder. Things were going well. But that summer, I got caught off guard with something I didn't see coming. One of the hip-hop gossip blogs published a report that I'd once worked as a correctional officer. They weaponized that information against me and used it to say I was a fraud and that my backstory was full of lies. All of a sudden, it seemed like the people were turning against me, and my career was in jeopardy.

That whole situation caught me flat-footed because this was something I'd never made an effort to conceal. This was something that people who knew me knew about, and it had never been an issue. Niggas in the streets knew what I was about. In Miami, there were zero questions about my credibility. If there had been, I promise you someone would have tried to step on my toes a long time ago, and they would have quickly found out what time it was. But that never happened.

But the streets and the internet are two very different places, and the way the blogs were spinning the story, Rick Ross was on the ropes. The attack on my character put me in survival mode. My defensive fight-or-flight instincts kicked in, and I reacted by claiming the rumors weren't true. That was a big mistake on my part, because when they brought the receipts out, it made the situation much worse. Now I'd been caught in a lie, and if I was lying about this, surely I must be lying about everything else.

Two months later, me and my crew ran into one of the bloggers that had been pushing the story. He got his ass beat down, and that felt good in the moment, but it most definitely wasn't worth all the time, energy and hundreds of thousands of dollars it took to put that situation behind me. My time and money are worth much more to me than any satisfaction I got from seeing a goofball get his eye socket caved in.

These days I deal with bloggers and paparazzi in a totally different way. Regardless of what they say, I don't get defensive. These people are just doing their jobs and their job is to use me to get ratings and clicks. But my job is to use them for my agenda. Who do you think wins that power struggle? Here's an exchange I had with a *TMZ* cameraman back in 2013.

TMZ: Rick, what's up, dude? How are you doing, bro?

Boss: Stop. I tell you the questions. That's Omarion. That's Stalley. That's Meek Mill. That's Rockie Fresh. You film what I tell you to film. *Self Made 3* is coming.

TMZ: Oh, congrats on that. I saw that on Instagram.

Boss: I know you did. But what about Wale's album? What day does that come out?

TMZ: June 26th?

Boss: No, the 25th. Don't mess that up no more. Now listen, when you see me, you film. You know why? Because I'm the biggest boss you've ever seen. You make sure they don't just play this video one time. You make sure they play this for a week straight.

The reality of the whole CO controversy was that I really never had anything to hide in the first place. I knew who I was and the code I'd lived by. I could have just explained the situation, and it would have been over with. The blogs could say whatever they wanted, but at the end of the day, the truth would prevail. My success would ultimately be determined by the quality of my music, not a part-time job I held for a year as a teenager. If I'd waited for the emotions of the situation to subside, instead of reacting hastily, I would have handled it much better. Emotions are always temporary. Decisions can have permanent effects.

A few years later, I lost a lucrative endorsement deal with Reebok following a controversy surrounding a bar on a song called "U.O.E.N.O." Once again, my first instinct was to go bad on the company for dropping me. But I'd learned from what had happened in 2008, so I gave myself some space to sit with it. I realized that Reebok had wanted to be in business with me. It was only due to my poor choice of words and bad judgment that this was no longer a viable partnership for a major corporation. Not only that, but if I'd gone on Twitter and said, "Fuck Reebok," I wouldn't have just burned a bridge with them. I would have probably scared off every other company that was considering partnering with me. Who would want to get into business with someone who may shit on them publicly if things go south? I would have made myself a liability. So I had to take responsibility for my actions and apologize to the people I'd offended and to my business partners, whom I'd put in a tough spot.

I fucked up again during a radio interview with *The Breakfast Club* in 2017. Angela Yee asked me why I didn't have any female artists signed to MMG, and I said it was because "I would end up fucking her and fucking the business up." There really wasn't any truth to that statement. It was an off-the-cuff comment, an attempt at being funny on a show looking for sound bites. But to all the women out there who knew they had to work twice as hard as men to achieve the same level of success, all while having to duck predatory Harvey Weinstein–type creep motherfuckers, my joke fell flat. Once again, I felt myself getting defensive.

Man, fuck this lame cancel culture bullshit, I thought. Anyone who actually knew me knew how much respect I have for women. The two most important players on my team are my momma and my sister. The people at my label who I work closest with are women. My manager's a woman. I got my start in the game ghostwriting for female artists. But once I got over my own ego and pride, I realized none of those things mattered. They were just excuses, and I already told you excuses don't mean shit. At the end of the day, I'd said something that was hurtful, and there was no reason I shouldn't own up to that.

I want to address an insensitive comment I made on a very sensitive issue, especially in a minority-dominated industry like hip-hop. My entire empire's backbone is led by two of the strongest people I know and they happen to be women, my mother and sister. The operations wouldn't run without them and I have the highest regard and respect for women in this industry. I have a daughter myself, my most cherished gift in the world.

My comment is not a reflection of my beliefs on the issue. A mistake I regret. I hope to use my mistake, my platform and the community to create positive discussion to implement change on a very important issue. Respect for the ones who stand up to say hey that isn't right. Now it's time to accept responsibility and do better.

I look forward to continuing to work with and support

female artists. My discovery process was documented by VH1 on Signed, *which premiered last night. Many of the most talented artists you'll see in the running to be the next MMG superstar are female artists. I look forward to clarifying my comments through my support. Thank you to everyone who's going through the journey with me. We're coming out every day stronger.*

Taking responsibility for your fuckups and opening yourself up to criticism is not something I saw a lot of growing up. That type of vulnerability is seen as weakness in the hood and people prey upon it. When you come into the rap game from the streets, you bring certain things with you, whether you're consciously aware of them or not. So it took me a minute to unlearn some of the things I'd been taught and make the switch from reactions to responses. I still listen to my gut, but most of the problems I face now are not life-and-death situations. More often than not, they are issues that would benefit from calm, well-thought-out responses. Responses come slower than reactions, but they're always based on more information.

CHAPTER

15

YOUR BEDROOM IS
YOUR OFFICE

Work is often seen as a means for making money so we can enjoy that second life that we lead. Even if we derive some satisfaction from our careers we still tend to compartmentalize our lives in this way. This is a depressing attitude, because in the end we spend a substantial part of our waking life at work. If we experience this time as something to get through on the way to real pleasure, then our hours at work represent a tragic waste of the short time we have to live.

—Robert Greene, *Mastery*

I WENT HOME LAST WEEK. BACK TO Clarksdale, Mississippi. The place where it all started for a young Rozay. Usually I go back pretty often. I've still got a lot of family in the area. But due to the pandemic, it had been a little while. I opted to make the six-hour drive rather than fly to make sure I didn't catch the fungus and bring it home to my momma. I like making that drive anyway. There ain't a whole lot to see, but riding past the old cotton fields and endless stretches of countryside reminds me how far I've come. I come from a long line of pecan pickers and real niggas. I wonder what the fuck my ancestors would make of me.

I made the trip for the grand opening of my newest Wingstop. Standing alongside my momma, my sister and Clarksdale's mayor, Chuck Espy, I cut the red ribbon with the blue oversized scissors, and then we all went in and celebrated with a ten-piece of lemon pepper wings. I didn't even have to ask them to separate the flats from the drums for me. They already knew my order.

I was now the proud owner of twenty-five Wingstops. But I was especially proud of this location. This one was special. Opening a business is hard enough under normal conditions, but to do it in the middle of a global pandemic requires a whole other level of hustling. I won't bore you with all the details of the planning and preparation that went into opening up this particular location, but just know that it was a three-year process.

Opening up a Wingstop in Clarksdale was deeper than just adding another asset to my portfolio. This was about bringing twenty new jobs to the city that birthed me. This was about taking a historic location that had been abandoned for years, Clarksdale's old Greyhound bus depot, and bringing it back to life as a Black-owned business. This was about showing the youth of Clarksdale how much they can rise above their humble beginnings and, when they do, not to forget where they came from and to give back. This was about buying back the block.

It's been ten years since I opened the doors to my first Wingstop in 2011. Aside from my music career, it's the only other venture I've been involved with for that long. It's incredible to see the results of a decade of consistent hard work, especially because Boss Wings LLC was not an overnight success. For the first few years, we were just trying to get out of the red and break even on our investment. Some of our first stores were poorly managed, and it took a lot to turn them around. Now those same stores that were struggling when we bought them bring in millions of dollars every year.

Boss Wings is a family-owned-and-operated enterprise, and I owe most of its success to my two partners: my momma, Ella, and my sister, Renee. They could explain to you all the nuts and bolts of the fast-food franchise game much better than I can. They're the ones who really work on the business plans, scout for potential new locations and recruit the amazing employees you find at our restaurants. My primary role has been marketing and promoting Wingstop. I think I've done a pretty good job at that.

She thinking Phillipe's, I'm thinking Wingstop
Fiending lemon pepper, I got my thing cocked
> —Rick Ross, "MC Hammer," *Teflon Don* (2010)

Waving at these bitches and I know these niggas ho-ish
Take your bitch to get lemon pepper in a new Lotus
> —Rick Ross, "King of Diamonds," *Rich Forever* (2012)

I hit a lick and went and bought a Wingstop (twenty of 'em)
I sprinkle lemon pepper in that re-rock (twenty of 'em)
> —Gucci Mane feat. Rick Ross, "Trap Boomin'," *I'm Up* (2012)

Wingstop owner, lemon pepper aroma
Young Black nigga, barely got a diploma
> —Rick Ross, "BLK & WHT," *Mastermind* (2014)

Tell the plug that I'm looking for an increase
Wingstop, Fatboy need a ten-piece

> —Rick Ross feat. Jay-Z, "The Devil Is a Lie,"
> *Mastermind* (2014)

I want it all, Wingstops on every corner
I want a mall, and I'm 'bout to build a Benihana

> —Rick Ross, "Bill Gates," *Black Dollar* (2015)

As soon as I opened my first store, Wingstop became integrated with everything else I had going on. Not just my lyrics. My music videos. My interviews. My photo shoots. My red-carpet appearances at award shows. Everything.

Repping Wingstop the way I do came very naturally to me. Because I was already a consumer of the product. I was eating lemon pepper ten-pieces way before I started selling them. So when I rep Wingstop in a song, it's not like I'm sitting in the studio with my notepad, trying to figure out how to insert some product placement in my raps to fulfill some contractual obligation. I have no such obligation. Wingstop is just a part of who I am now. So rapping about eating lemon pepper comes as easily to me as talking about driving a couple of bricks up to Jacksonville.

Having that genuine love for a product is one of my requirements for partnering up with a brand. It has to be something I love personally. Whenever I see a celebrity endorse a product, I can always tell if they're in it strictly for the check. You see them do the commercial or the sponsored post on social media, and that's really the only time you ever see them repping. It's as if they're embarrassed that they even have to do it. There's always a very clear line between their artistry and their "work."

That's never been me. I've always subscribed to the philosophy that the way you do one thing is the way you do everything. Even when I was thirteen years old working at the car wash in Carol City making $30 a day, I always went above and beyond what was expected of me. I was always willing to go a little further than everybody else. After I finished washing a car, vacuuming the interior and degreasing the seats, I'd go through the cassettes and CDs and arrange them in alphabetical order. Part of me did it for tips. But the truth is, I would have put in the same amount of effort even if there were no tips involved. I just like the feeling of doing a great job at whatever it is I'm doing. Mobb Deep said there ain't no such thing as halfway crooks, and Rozay says there ain't no such thing as halfway hustlers. I have no interest in being mediocre or decent at anything. I want to be the best in the world at everything I do. If you want to be great, then be great twenty-four hours a day, seven days a week, 365 days a year. If you want to go hard, then always go hard.

I take as much pride in all of my business ventures as

I do in my music. I go so hard for Wingstop that people sometimes mistake me for the CEO of the company. I'm not. That title belongs to Charlie Morrison. But even though I'm just a humble franchise owner, I don't only promote my locations. I promote every Wingstop. I'm proud to be in business with Wingstop, and what's good for the goose is good for the gander. Now I'm just waiting for Charlie Morrison to post a picture of my next album cover. I know it's only a matter of time before he does it.

I'm about my paper, but I'm not a transactional person. What I mean is when I do something, I don't just do the bare minimum that's required of me to get what I want in return. I put my all into everything I do. If you do more than what you're paid for, eventually you will be paid for more than what you do.

That's a lot easier to do when you have genuine affection for what you're doing and don't really view it as work. When I decided to expand my franchise game beyond Wingstop and bought a Checkers, I bought the one me and my teammates used to go to get cheeseburgers at after our high school football games. So it's not a chore for me to promote that that's my restaurant. That place really means something to me.

I'm involved in a lot of shit. So I can see how someone might assume that I just say yes to every paid opportunity that comes my way. That might be the case when it comes to getting booked for shows or paid features, but those are things that I love doing and will always align with my brand. Believe it or not, when it comes to brand partnerships, I think I'm pretty selective. I say no much more often than I say yes.

Earlier when I was talking about Holyfield, I mentioned how I see one of the reasons he lost his fortune was through his failed businesses outside of the sport of boxing. Like me, Holyfield had his name attached to a long list of brands and products. So what was the difference? Why did the same play that led to Holyfield's downfall result in me making millions of dollars? I'll tell you why. They weren't the same play.

Holyfield was a highly decorated Olympic medalist and four-time world heavyweight champion. In a violent sport full of cold-blooded killers, he was the consummate churchgoing nice guy who didn't drink, smoke or talk trash. He most definitely had a distinct brand. He just never capitalized on it properly.

Holyfield was known as one of the best-trained and best-conditioned athletes in the sport. So he should have been selling workout equipment and protein powder instead of hawking barbecue sauce and fire extinguishers. He claimed to be a devout born-again Christian, so why did he launch a record label and sign a gangster rapper who was C-Murder's protégé? Why would anyone look to Evander Holyfield for these things?

I got into wine and spirits because alcohol and partying go hand in hand with the nightlife scene that I'm involved in every weekend. I started a fast-food franchise enterprise because people know Rozay is a fat nigga who loves to eat good. I have my own line of beard oil because I have the most stunning beard in the history of beards. I became a partner in a sports agency because people know I was a heavily recruited high school football player. Everything I do is consistent with who I am. That's why my ventures have all been successful.

The decisions I make in business are based on what motivates me and inspires me. The amount of money I may make comes second to that. I work on things I'm passionate about so I never have to feel like I'm at work. When you stop viewing work as something you have to do, versus something you look forward to, you get different results. Hustling hard is always an opportunity, never an obligation. Don't think that you put in long hours at the office so you can come home and enjoy being in bed. When you can find a way to enjoy every aspect of your life, even when you're in the trenches, that's when you've truly mastered the game. Your bedroom is your office.

CHAPTER

16

BOSSES STAY
STUDENTS

TWENTY-FIVE WINGSTOPS IN, YOU MIGHT think that I know all there is to know about the fast-food franchise game. You'd be mistaken. I could own two hundred fifty restaurants and I wouldn't feel that way. I've still got a lot to learn. A real boss always remains a student, regardless of how successful they've been doing things a certain way. They know they don't have it all figured out and that they will always have to discover new ways to innovate and evolve with the times. A boss doesn't cling to the past. They welcome the changing of the tide.

Wingstop had been booming throughout the pandemic. The company's stock price was under $50 in March, and by July, it was up to damn near $150. Unfortunately for me, I own very little Wingstop stock. I missed out on that opportunity to triple up. I never really got into stocks, bonds and mutual funds. I have no idea what cryptocurrency is. I think that comes from how I was raised. Growing up, I saw my parents invest their savings in real estate. They didn't believe in 401(k)s or IRAs. They wanted their money to have a physical address. They wanted to know exactly where it was, and they wanted to be able to touch it. Naturally I ended up inheriting that mindset.

I like investing in real estate because I've never lost money in it. It's not the biggest profit margins, but it's steady and reliable. Having that stable growth allows me to take bigger risks in other ventures. That way when I partner up with an early stage brand, instead of taking a bigger payday up front, I can accept less in the short term in exchange for some equity in the business. Remember what I said earlier. If it ain't a long-term play, then it's just small talk.

But the way Wingstop's stock was jumping made me reconsider. I might be missing out on some easy money. I felt the same way about the Bitcoin shit. If my ignorance was resulting in me leaving money on the table, I could at least try to become more informed. It didn't mean I suddenly had to switch up my whole investment strategy. I could just expand my knowledge and go from there. The smarter you are, the better your chances at winning are going to be.

Avoid complacency. The moment you start thinking you've got the game all figured out, you set a ceiling for yourself. If you maintain a beginner's mindset, then you're always learning. If you're always learning, you're always improving. If you want to keep winning, you're going to have to find new ways to win. You can't lean on your past victories to earn your next ones. You have to look ahead toward the future.

When it comes to my music, I always try to work with up-and-coming artists and producers. I may have more plaques and paper than them, but the younger generation are the ones who are on the cutting edge of what's happening in music. Me working with them helps me keep my music from becoming outdated. I believe that's a big part of the reason why I'm still relevant in the game after all these years.

In 2010, I was on the set of Waka Flocka Flame's music video for his breakout single, "O Let's Do It," when I heard another buzzing record of his called "Hard in da Paint." It was produced by a nineteen-year-old beat maker by the name of Lex Luger. It was unlike anything on the radio at the time, and it immediately got my attention. His beats were menacing and mean. Up until then, my signature sound had been what I call the "Maybach sound," luxurious beats with live instrumentation and expensive soulful samples. Lex Luger's beats sounded like they took ten minutes to make, which they actually did. I sensed his style of production was going to have a moment, and I wanted to be at the forefront of it. If I'd been closed off to the idea of making different kinds of records and switching up my style, you would have never gotten my second signature sound. You would have never gotten records from me like "B.M.F." and "MC Hammer," or mixtapes like *Albert Anastasia* and *Rich Forever*. My willingness to learn new things and adapt to changing times is why I've remained relevant in the culture after all these years.

I love making music, and I know I still have a lot more classic records left in me. But I also recognize that hip-hop is a young man's game, and the youth aren't going to be checking for my next album when I'm fifty years old the same way they are today. That's just the way this hip-hop shit goes. Ten years from now, the youngsters aren't going to know what the fuck I'm talking about when I say, "M.I. Yayo."

Look at Jay-Z. Hov is still a dope MC. He hasn't lost a step musically. But these days he makes headlines more for his business moves than his albums. He was smart enough to recognize that his time as the hottest artist in the industry wouldn't last forever, and so when he was at his peak, he started to look beyond music and lay the groundwork so that he could reinvent himself and transition into an even more successful chapter of his career as a businessman.

I've taken the same approach. The moment I established myself as the top artist in the game is when I started to branch out and began the process of setting myself up for the inevitable moment when someone else came along and claimed that spot. That person was probably Drake. And after Drake, it'll be someone else. Nothing lasts forever, and that's why you need to always keep learning and growing.

I was never a strong student in school. I always struggled academically. Instead of trying to work through those difficulties, I took on the role of the class clown. I think a lot of kids do that. I put on a front like I didn't care about my education. But that was never the truth. I had highly intelligent and educated parents. I always wanted to bring home good grades like my sister.

As I got older, I began to embrace my education. It's been of tremendous benefit to me, not only in business, but also in my relationships with my friends and family members. Keeping an open mind and knowing that I don't know everything has opened a lot of doors for me.

I was excited to bring a beginner's mindset to a new venture. A week after my visit to Clarksdale, I announced the launch of Collins Ave Cannabis. Rozay was finally in the weed game. Well, that's not exactly true. I actually had a lengthy history in the weed game. But I was finally in the *legal* weed game. This was a move I'd wanted to make for years, but due to the case I caught in 2015, I'd had to put those plans on the back burner. It turns out trying to sell weed when you're in the middle of fighting a case in a state where it's still illegal isn't the best look. My attorney advised me against it, and I took that advice. But as soon as I completed the terms of my probation, I made my move.

I was launching Collins Ave Cannabis in partnership with the biggest brand in the industry: Berner's Cookies. We decided to start off with three strains: Collins

Ave is an indica. Lemon Pepper is a spicy sativa. And Pink Rozay is a hybrid. All three are fantastic, but if you're an all-day smoker like myself, I recommend starting out with the Pink Rozay.

As soon as the opportunity with Cookies presented itself, I was in. I didn't care if there was a bigger offer on the table from one of Berner's competitors. I didn't need to hear those offers. If I was interested in a straightforward licensing play and just slapping my handsome mug on a loud pack, I would have explored my options. But what I was interested in was learning how to build a vertically integrated cannabis company from the ground up, and I knew there was no better person to partner up with for that than Berner. When Berner and I first crossed paths in the early 2000s, Berner was a budtender at a dispensary in San Francisco. Now he's the founder and CEO of a company that's worth over a half billion dollars. His shops bring in hundreds of thousands of dollars every day. What he's accomplished with Cookies is unbelievable.

When I was growing up in Miami, a lot of the weed I smoked was garbage shit that people grew in their backyards. Early on when I started selling it, I came into possession of several pounds that me and my homies named "Headbanga Boogie" because that junk gave you a headache. Miami was the cocaine capital, but when it came to cannabis, my city had a lot to learn. Once I started traveling to the West Coast, I fell in love with the high-quality weed they had out there.

What Berner did with Cookies in California is what I wanted Collins Ave Cannabis to be for the South. This partnership made that possible. Cookies was in possession of one of Florida's coveted twenty-two medical marijuana licenses, so that was my foot in the door. I knew I wasn't going to have a half-billion-dollar brand overnight. It took Berner twenty years to get Cookies to where it's at. Florida is a long way from legalizing recreational marijuana, so this was going to be a long-term endeavor, and that was okay because I knew with certainty that my passion for smoking good weed wasn't going anywhere.

I'm blessed Berner believes in me and is willing to share his blueprint for building a cannabis empire. You know how many rappers want to launch their own strain, let alone three, under the Cookies banner? I'll tell you. Every single rapper you can think of. So I was honored and excited about the partnership. It felt like I just signed my first record deal.

Bosses stay students, and having that beginner's mindset will take you far. This is a fast-paced world, and things are constantly changing. If you're stuck in your ways and can't learn, adapt and evolve, you're going to end up like the megalodon shark. Extinct.

CHAPTER
17

SPEAK IT INTO EXISTENCE

I am the greatest. I said that even before I knew I was. Don't tell me I can't do something. Don't tell me it's impossible. Don't tell me I'm not the greatest. I'm the double greatest.

—Muhammad Ali

MY JEWISH BROTHER FROM CHICAGO CAME to see me. Brett Berish. He brought the whole Luc Belaire squad with him, so it was a family affair. It felt good to see everyone again. We spent a few days doing photo shoots at The Promise Land and got a lot of dope new content. Assets we could use to continue promoting our brands throughout the pandemic.

Brett is the founder and CEO of Sovereign Brands, the parent company behind Luc Belaire, Bumbu, McQueen and the Violet Fog, Villon, among several other wine and spirits brands. He and I have been business partners and close friends for almost a decade now, ever since DJ Clue slid me a bottle of Luc Belaire one night while I was performing at a club in New York City. I loved the taste, but what I was first drawn to was the look of the bottle: black with neon-pink lettering. I'd never seen anything quite like it.

"What is this?" I asked Clue.

"Luc Belaire," he told me. "It's new. It's from the same guy who Jay-Z partnered up with on Armand de Brignac."

I knew Hov was making a killing with his Ace of

Spades, and I also knew he was highly selective when it came to who he did business with. If he had partnered with this Brett guy, that was a strong cosign. I'd been wanting to make a move into wine and spirits. My first ever endorsement deal was with 1800 Tequila back in 2009. A few years later, I became a brand ambassador for Puff's Cîroc Vodka. I made a good chunk of change with both, but neither of those things were really mine. I was now at a point in my career where I was more interested in having a piece of a company than just getting a check for promoting someone else's shit. So I asked DJ Clue to make the introduction.

Brett made a strong impression on me from the jump. As soon as I met him, I realized he was different from most of the middle-aged white guys I'd encountered in my dealings with corporate America. He most definitely didn't look like your average CEO. He had long white hair and a beard that was as big as mine. He had a bunch of bohemian-style necklaces around his neck. He looked like a shepherd or the leader of a cult movement. This motherfucker looked like David Koresh. But it wasn't just his physical appearance that made Brett stand out. His whole energy was a refreshing change of pace.

To give you some context, Brett and I first met in 2012. My stock was at an all-time high, and I was *the* biggest star in the rap game. I'm not being hyperbolic. I'm strictly speaking facts. I'd just topped MTV's "Hottest MCs in the Game" list. *The Source* had named me "Man of the Year" for the second year in a row. My fifth album, *God Forgives, I Don't*, had just done the biggest first-week sales of my career.

I say all of that to say that every corporate white guy I crossed paths with at this time wanted to be in business with me. But Brett played it real cool. He wasn't trying to sell me on anything or convince me of what he had to offer. Keep in mind that this was in 2012. He was just genuinely excited to meet a fan of his new brand.

"I heard you like the packaging," he said. "You know, everyone said we were crazy for the black bottle. They told me, 'You can't see the liquid! People won't even be able to see the bottle in a dark nightclub!'"

"It's beautiful."

"They also said I was crazy for starting out with a sparkling rosé. In the sparkling wine category, most brands start out with a brut before introducing other cuvées."

I was pretty green when it came to sparkling wine. I had no idea that sparkling wine was only considered champagne if the grapes came from the Champagne region of France. Luc Belaire was a sparkling rosé from the Provence-Alpes-Côte d'Azur region of France. It turned out that point of distinction made Luc Belaire more affordable than a bottle of Dom Pérignon.

That was appealing to me. I'd assumed Luc Belaire

must cost $300 a bottle. The product was such high quality. I loved that this was a premium wine at a reasonable price point.

I remember when I first started hitting the clubs in Miami as a teenager. This was way before anyone was letting me into any VIP section. I would look past the bouncers and red velvet ropes that separated me from all the baddest hoes and the dope boys who were getting money. They were all drinking Cristal. The gold bottles looked like trophies. They stood for something. They were symbols of their success. Meanwhile, I was on the other side, holding a plastic cup of some brown liquor. I wanted to be in the VIP section drinking the good stuff. But I just wasn't there yet.

When I discovered that Luc Belaire wasn't totally out of a young hustler's price range, I was even more intrigued. Between the price point, the packaging and the taste, Luc Belaire was checking all the boxes. This was something I wanted to get involved in.

To my surprise, Brett wasn't ready to do a deal with me just yet. It would be another year before we entered into an official partnership on paper. Despite the fact that Brett and I had hit it off, he didn't want to rush into anything prematurely. He had just launched Luc Belaire. Like a true sommelier, Brett wanted to let Luc Belaire breathe and develop its own identity before letting the biggest boss become the face of it. I understood where he was coming from, but I had my own agenda. I was determined to manifest it into reality.

Most people assume I got into business with Luc Belaire much earlier than I actually did. Because for the next year, I repped Luc Belaire with no financial stake whatsoever. And I repped it hard. Brett would hook me up with free cases and I had bottles sent out to all my contacts in the music industry, with a note telling them this was Rozay's favorite rosé. Just like I'd done with Wingstop, I made it a part of everything I had going on. I rapped about it in my music and featured it in my videos. These were the early days of Instagram and I encouraged my followers to rep it with me using the hashtags #BlackBottleBoys and #BlackBottleGirls. We got Black Bottle Boys letterman jackets made and everyone wanted to get their hands on those. Those jackets became the equivalent of those gold Cristal bottles back in the day. Status symbols.

305 the realest, Ricky Ross the richest
Belaire on my table, I talk it then I live it
—DJ Khaled feat. Rick Ross, "I Feel Like Pac/I Feel Like Biggie," *Suffering from Success* (2013)

Bow down to the biggest, Belaire I be spilling
Counting all this paper, no games with these pussy niggas
—Rick Ross feat. Future, "No Games," *Mastermind* (2014)

Black bottle and a bad bitch
Club Armani where the cash is

—Rick Ross feat. Jay-Z, "The Devil Is a Lie,"
Mastermind (2014)

Believing and speaking things into existence is something I've practiced as far back as I can remember. One of the first songs I ever wrote was called "Where the Hoes At?" which I wrote with my homie Bishop. We were in the third grade at the time. "Where the Hoes At?" was Bishop and me bragging about all our exploits with all the finest females at Miami's five main Black high schools. Of course, we had experienced none of those exploits. We were nine-year-old virgins still in elementary school. But we knew where we wanted to get to, and so we rapped from that perspective.

The way I promoted my John Deere tractor earlier in this book, you might assume they were sponsoring all the landscaping costs at The Promise Land. They're not yet. But I look forward to doing business with them in the future. Just wait and see. I will be acknowledged as a successful Black farmer. I've already planted the seed. It's only a matter of time before my crops come into harvest, and when they do, I highly recommend you preorder the limited-edition John Deere x Rick Ross tractor because they're going to sell out fast.

I look forward to doing business with John Deere. I look forward to owning a piece of a sports franchise.

I look forward to partnering with automobile manufacturers and airlines. You can achieve the seemingly impossible through self-belief and sheer force of will.

Speak your dreams into existence. Don't take no for an answer. When someone closes one door in your face, keep ringing the doorbell until they have no choice but to let you in. Or try the back door. Climb through the window if you have to. Or like Khaled says, "Rip the door off and then put the hinges in the haters' hands."

It's been eight years since Brett and I first crossed paths, and our partnership is as strong as ever. Luc Belaire is the top-selling French rosé in the United States and the fastest-growing one in the world. The brand has more than 1.5 million followers across official social media accounts and fan-made ones. Our online presence is equivalent to the three largest brands in the champagne category combined. We've added four more bottles to the range: Belaire Deluxe, Belaire Brut Gold, Belaire Luxe Rosé and Belaire Bleu. We've expanded into rum, gin and cognac. Sovereign Brands is a privately held company and Brett would kill me if I spilled the beans on how much money we've made together, so I'll just leave it at this. It's a mind-blowing amount.

I'm proud of our accomplishments, but there's still work to be done. Especially now. Ever since the start of the pandemic, all the clubs have been shut down, and all nightlife has been put on hold indefinitely. The clubs have been a major point of sale for Luc Belaire.

Sipping a glass of Luc Belaire is an on-premise experience. What that means is it's a product people generally consume at the same place that they purchase it.

The nightlife scene is also where I promote Luc Belaire heavily. When I get booked for a club appearance, the promoters know to have the VIP section stocked with black bottles. They know they need to have thirty bottle girls holding the light-up bottles with the sparklers. So when I go city to city, not only do I get paid to perform, I hit the club and drive up sales of Luc Belaire in every market.

But business as usual wasn't going to work for the moment we were living in. We had to get creative and start thinking outside the box.

First, we had to expand our retail presence. Early on in the pandemic, I doubled up on promoting Luc Belaire and Bumbu on my social media. When people woke up and checked their IG, I wanted the first thing they saw to be me eating my breakfast omelet in between two bottles of Belaire. That became my morning routine, and I started calling the segment "Belaire Tower," where I would speak to my fans and give them some inspirational boss talk or start up some controversy by talking shit about one of my adversaries. When the blogs picked it up and reposted, that was free promo for my brands. All of it was subliminal messaging. I was subtly communicating that Luc Belaire was something to have on deck at the crib for morning mimosas and

Bumbu for evening nightcaps. These weren't just for weekend nights at the club. Once again, I was manifesting my vision into existence.

A few months into the pandemic, Brett hit me up and asked if he and I could hop on a Vroom call for a strategic planning meeting. I didn't know what he was talking about, so I hit him on FaceTime instead.

"Brett, what the fuck is a Vroom call?" I asked.

"It's actually called Zoom, and if you could have someone help you install it on your computer, that would be great. I'm going to send you some AirPods too. I think we're going to be doing a lot of video conference calls for the foreseeable future."

I installed the Zoom software, and Brett and I got on a call. Then he let me know the new play.

"Okay, Rick. So, retail is the life of the industry now, and our retail presence is primarily independent stores. The mom-and-pop shops. We need to find a way to support them, because a lot of these small businesses are really hurting right now."

"Most definitely."

"I had a feeling you might say that. So what I want to start doing is having these video conference calls with our distributors and retail accounts across the country. So we can strengthen those relationships and find out what assets we can provide them with to help them promote their stores. Merchandising displays and things like that. I also think you being on there and sharing your story of overcoming hardship and achieving success will be really inspiring and motivating to these people."

"I'm with it," I said. "I can even record some shout-outs to the different stores that they can use to promote their stores, and I can record ones for their employees of the month to boost morale."

"That's a great idea. The only thing is these calls may not be the most glamorous events. I really can't even tell you how many people will be on them."

"Well, even if there's just one person on there, then it's worth it," I told him.

"I really appreciate you, Rick. You already do so much, and I know this is outside the scope of your usual duties."

"Brett, I'll be on every Vroom call for as long as it takes. Just let me know what you need from me and I'll make it happen."

CHAPTER
18

LET YOUR ACTIONS
SPEAK FOR YOU

I GET MESSAGES ALL THE TIME FROM PEOPLE asking if they can work for me. The first thing I look to see is if they're already working for me. Are they posting my new single and the cover art for my upcoming album? Are they repping my brands? I better not check your page and find a photo of you in the club holding up a bottle of anything other than Luc Belaire or Bumbu. That's an easy way to lose my attention. You might even get blocked for something like that. You know I can be a petty motherfucker.

When "Hustlin'" was taking off, I started to hear about a DJ over at Diamonds Cabaret in Miami who was playing my breakout single back to back to back. Rumor was this person had played my record so many times, he got suspended from the strip club. I'd never been to Diamonds, and I wasn't familiar with the DJs who worked there, so I asked my manager, E-Class, who he'd paid there to promote "Hustlin'." He had no idea what I was talking about.

Eventually I came to learn that the DJ was Sam Sneak. I knew Sam a little bit from running into him in different clubs over the years. He was a cool young Haitian brother who loved two things: music and sneakers. I liked Sam, but at that time we most definitely didn't have the type of close friendship where I would expect him to put his job on the line for me and ask for nothing in return. That meant something. Sam's been my official DJ and one of the most important members of my team ever since.

Don't just tell me you want to work for me. Show me. That goes for whatever it is you want in life. When you approach opportunities with your hand out like a beggar asking to get put on without bringing anything to the table, you're doing the bare minimum. That's level one hustling. Amateur hour. Anyone can do that. Separate yourself from the average amateurs. Instead of having to explain yourself, be assertive and take actions that demonstrate your value. Don't ask for an opportunity. Make yourself a can't-miss opportunity for someone else. Be the one with something to offer.

Why haven't you put MMG Brand Ambassador in your bio and gotten to work already? Didn't I already tell you to manifest your goals into existence in the last chapter? What exactly is it that you're waiting on to get started?

To be clear, I'm not looking to get free labor out of anyone. I believe people should be compensated fairly for their work. Trust me when I say I don't *need* you to be rubbing Rich by Rick Ross beard oil on your face for your fifty-seven followers on TikTok. What I'm looking for is initiative.

If you're a young entrepreneur with a clothing line, pack me up a care package and send that shit to the crib. I wear XXL. It takes two seconds to look up my address. I have the most famous house in the state of Georgia. Fuck it, I'll save you the two seconds. It's 794 Evander Holyfield Highway. They haven't changed it to Rozay Road yet, but you better believe it's only a matter of time before they do.

I received a lot of these packages during the pandemic, and I always show love. If your shit is fly, I'm going to wear it. If it's not, I'll probably still post it to my story just because I respect the hustle. I get offers to rep brands for lots of money every day, but I love shining a light on the young hustlers who might not have the funds for a sponsored post from Rozay just yet. If they're showing love and repping my shit, I'm going to give it back.

The reason I can have such high expectations of people is because I hold myself to the same high standard. Remember, when I first met Brett, he wasn't ready to bring me on as a partner in Luc Belaire. Maybe the timing wasn't right, like he says. Or maybe he had some other reservations about me that I didn't know about. It doesn't matter what his reasoning was. What mattered was that I didn't sit around with my fingers crossed waiting for Brett to maybe hopefully one day change his mind. I took control of the situation and of my destiny. I went out and started repping Luc Belaire like I already had a stake in it. And I did it at a time when deals were being brought to me on a silver platter every day. Why would I do that? The answer is simple. I am a highly visual person, and I had a specific vision that involved Brett's black bottles. I was going to bring that vision to life, and I didn't care what it took.

I know what you might be wondering. What if it hadn't all come together in the end? What if I put in all the "free labor" promoting Luc Belaire and it never paid off? Is it better to play things safe? Is betting big on yourself a risk worth taking? To me, it is. Because I can live with the disappointment of putting my all into something and coming up short. It's a hard pill to swallow, but I can digest it. Even if my hard work doesn't get the results I wanted, I can hold my head high knowing that I went after what I wanted. I know if I just keep moving forward, eventually things are going to go my way. What I can't live with are the regrets of not even trying because I was afraid of it not working out. Those regrets are the things that eat at your soul and keep you up at night, and I already have enough difficulty sleeping as it is.

I spend very little time worrying about "What if it goes wrong?" Instead I focus on "What if it goes right?" When it does, trust me, you're going to make back whatever your initial investment in yourself was and then a whole lot more. When it all comes together and all those early mornings and late nights pay off, that's when you're going to see the confetti start to fall from the sky. Poof!

By the time Brett and I made our partnership official, there were very little negotiations to be had. There were no questions about the value I was going to bring to Sovereign Brands because I had already gone out and demonstrated my value. Do you know what that meant for me? It meant that this deal wasn't going to go down like on *Shark Tank*, where the entrepreneur says they're worth one amount and then Mark Cuban says, "No, you're actually worth much less than that." My valuation was rock-solid. Which meant I got everything I was looking for. It was the biggest deal for the biggest boss. A max contract. It was a win-win for everyone involved. At that point, there was only one thing left for Brett and me to do. We signed on the dotted line, poured us some Luc Belaire and raised our glasses for a toast.

L'chaim!

CHAPTER
19

HUSTLE YOUR OWN WAY

Watchin' Kanye interview, feel like I wanna cry
For every innocent brother charged with a homicide
Went from battle raps to now we wearing MAGA hats
Dade County, nigga, mansions up in Tamarac
Never golfing with the Trumps and I give you my word
Back to coming out the trunk, charging twenty a bird

—Rick Ross, "Vegas Residency," *Port of Miami II* (2019)

I GOT A PHONE CALL FROM KANYE WEST'S people telling me that the Louis Vuitton Don was in Atlanta and wanted to see me. Kanye was nearby at Pinewood Atlanta, a seven-hundred-acre film studio in Fayetteville. Atlanta has become a major filmmaking mecca in recent years, and Pinewood is where they shot all the big Marvel superhero movies, like *The Avengers* and *Black Panther*. Kanye had flown his whole team down from Wyoming and set up shop in Stage 17, the studio's biggest soundstage. I put on a gray camel-hair Balenciaga sweater, hopped in my Phantom and made my way over.

I was pulling up on Kanye with some skepticism. For as long as I've known him—close to twenty years now—my dawg has been ruffling people's feathers in one way or another. It's what people love and hate about Kanye. It wasn't until recently that his antics ever rubbed me the wrong way. That started around the time he came out in support of Donald Trump for president and started saying things like slavery was a choice.

These days Kanye was singing a slightly different

tune. He'd apparently lost faith in Trump and decided that he should be the president instead. He was still saying a lot of foul shit. Like that Harriet Tubman never freed the slaves and that vaccines were the mark of the beast. That chemicals in deodorant and toothpaste were preventing people from being in service to God. Just a few days earlier he'd gone on one of his lengthy Twitter rants where he said he wanted to divorce Kim Kardashian because she was trying to get him "locked up like Nelson Mandela."

Kanye was acting ocky. There was no doubt about that. But he and I had a history together, and I'm not the type of person who ends friendships over tweets. Especially because I wasn't totally clear on what was really going on. At the same time Kanye was saying all this weirdo goofy shit, he had also just donated $2 million to the families of George Floyd, Ahmaud Arbery and Breonna Taylor. There were a lot of contradictions, and things weren't adding up. I knew Kanye had been open about being bipolar, so maybe my brother was going through some mental health shit.

It had been a few years since I'd last seen Kanye face-to-face, and I wasn't sure why he wanted to see me. At first I was thinking maybe he needed somewhere in Atlanta to host one of his Sunday Services. The Promise Land would most definitely be a beautiful place for that. Or maybe he wanted to get my support for his presidential campaign. I had my own reasons for going. I was working on a new album, *Richer Than I Ever Been*, and I needed some of that classic soulful Kanye West production.

I remember being blown away when Kanye invited me to Hawaii in 2010 to be a part of his fifth album, *My Beautiful Dark Twisted Fantasy*. I'd never been in one studio with so many elite rappers, producers and engineers at the same time. They called it "Rap Camp." This situation he had going on at Pinewood Studios was equally impressive, but it was on a totally different type of vibe.

After getting past security—it was like Fort Knox to get in that bitch—I was greeted at the entrance by Kanye's longtime manager, John Monopoly, and then, to my surprise, retired NBA player Rick Fox. That was a curveball. I always knew Rick Fox to be a reliable small forward. I'd had no idea his career after basketball involved working for Kanye West.

Kanye showed up a few minutes later with an older white gentleman. We couldn't embrace properly due to the social distancing, but it was all love between us. Kanye seemed like himself. Despite his erratic tweets, there was no indication that he was in the middle of some type of manic episode.

I recognized the man standing next to him. It was Dan Cathy, the chairman and CEO of Chick-fil-A. Being in the fast-food business myself, I've always made it a point to familiarize myself with the power brokers in the industry. Regardless of what field you're in, you want to be in the know as to who's running shit. You can learn from their successes as well as their mistakes and apply those lessons to your own hustle.

What I hadn't known was that Dan Cathy was also the owner of Pinewood Studios. This motherfucker was really rich. He and Kanye had built a friendship rooted in their shared religious beliefs, which was how Ye had gotten plugged in with the studio's biggest soundstage.

"It's nice to meet you, Rick," Dan said. "So, are you and Kanye good friends?"

Kanye cut in before I could respond.

"Oh yes, we're very good friends, Dan. As a matter of fact, Rick and I used to rap in front of hotels together."

"Wow... Well, that's interesting."

Dan left a couple of minutes later, and Kanye started giving us the lay of the land. He'd relocated his entire operation—his music, his sneaker and clothing lines, as well as his presidential campaign—to this one forty-thousand-square-foot space.

"The way the room is set up is based on how all these things are all organized in my brain," he explained. "Excuse me, can we send a photographer to the top of that ladder for a bird's-eye view from overhead? I'd really like for Rick to see what the inside of my brain looks like."

"We've only been here four days and we're already running out of space," Rick Fox added. "If we're going to stay past September, Dan says we may have to move to one of the smaller stages."

"That's strike two with these people," Kanye said. "You want to know what strike one was?"

"Of course," I replied.

"Strike one was when I requested the circular tables and it took over an hour for them to arrive. Guess who I called during that hour?"

"I can only imagine."

"Tyler Perry! Because he's the only other Black man I know who's made movies here! I said, 'Tyler, how long am I supposed to wait for my circular tables?'"

"And how long did he say?"

"He didn't know, but he said that these are good people that work here and that I shouldn't take the table situation personally."

"That makes sense."

"I know. I really just wanted to let Tyler know I was here in his city, and that was my way of reaching out to tell him that."

I wasn't sure how to respond to that one. Luckily the conversation shifted as Rick Fox continued the tour and brought us over to the Yeezy apparel and footwear area. There were rows of sewing machines and geometric color-coded piles of clothing and sneakers everywhere. It looked like a sweatshop.

Kanye's sneaker deal with Adidas had recently made him a billionaire, and he was about to make a whole lot more money through a recently announced clothing partnership with GAP. That was if he didn't talk himself out of it. Despite his tremendous success in the fashion world, Kanye was frustrated.

"I'm not on the board of directors at Adidas, and I'm not on the board of GAP either. Do you know what that is?!" he asked. "It's white supremacy!"

Then he leaned in and whispered something else to me.

"Tell me, Rick... Do you think Jeff Bezos would agree to these deals?!"

This kept happening during my visit. Kanye would have my attention and he'd be onto something, but then he would lose me. As far as Adidas, I could wrap my mind around what he was saying. He did this deal, and it turned out to be a way bigger success than anyone probably imagined, and now he wanted more. More money, a seat on the board, whatever. I understood that. I've had to restructure my contracts as my value increased. But what I couldn't understand was how he just did this deal with GAP two months ago and he was already yelling about the white supremacy and Jeff Bezos. If having a seat on the board was so important to Kanye, why didn't he demand it while they were negotiating the terms of their arrangement? I'm sure they could have made a spot for him on the board.

I couldn't remember the last time I saw a nigga in a GAP sweatshirt. GAP's stock price had soared upon the news of their partnership. Kanye was about to turn that whole company up. I doubt they would let him walk away over something like that. I just didn't understand how he could agree to a deal and then start going crazy over it two days later. That shit just didn't make any sense to me.

The tour concluded with a presentation on Kanye's presidential campaign. Standing in front of a one-hundred-foot screen that featured an American flag flapping in the wind, Kanye explained his "2020 Vision." God is love. Jesus. White supremacy. Christian TikTok. Recycling. Yeezy igloos. Honestly, I tuned out during most of it. But something he said afterward got my attention.

"Tomorrow I might tweet that I don't feel like being president anymore," he said.

"It's going to get a million retweets," one of his campaign staffers responded.

That's when it all hit me. I'd been trying to make sense of Kanye's erratic behavior, because after all, the man was worth a billion, and that was what I was working toward. So I had to be missing something. But the answer had been right in front of my face the entire time. This was the whole fucking play. Kanye wasn't successful in spite of his ockyness. The ockyness was the whole point. Fake running for president.

Fake going crazy on Twitter. The ugly foam slides. The clothes were ugly on purpose. All of this shit was for attention, and it really didn't matter if it was positive or negative attention because his brand grew either way. That's why he liked Donald Trump. That's why he loved the Kardashians. It all made sense now.

When Kanye and I were rapping in front of hotels in 2002, we were on a similar mission. Young, hungry and hopeful that our work ethic and the quality of our music would lead to fame and fortune. But this was a new chapter of Kanye's career, and now everything was strictly about shock value. That was why he was now making songs called "Scoopity Poop." Say what you want to say about it, but the strategy was working out well for him. Kanye could spend $10 million on advertising—for his campaign, his album, his clothes, whatever he wanted to promote—and that would last a weekend. But if he went on Twitter and called Kris Jenner "Kris Jong-Un," that shit would be covered by every news outlet for weeks for free. It all made sense now. Kanye had mastered the art of ocky manipulation. I was fucked-up. Was this what I needed to be doing? Was this the way for me to ascend to the billionaires' club?

Everyone's blueprint for success is different. I know TikTok and Triller are the youngsters' new favorite social media platforms and I can respect that. I don't want to be an out-of-touch, old motherfucker, but at the

same time, if I was on those apps doing "The Woah"
and shaking my ass, I feel like that would be out of
touch. I need to do what works for me. Chick-fil-A is
one of the most successful fast-food chains in the country, and there's a lot that I could learn from taking a
peek at Dan Cathy's playbook. But that doesn't mean
I need to start closing all my Wingstops on Sundays.

Study the strategies of others and, by all means, bor-
row from them when it suits your interests. But make
sure you're still on your own path, one that's aligned
with your authentic self and your own code of principles. It's easy to fall into the trap of thinking that the
way another person is winning is the only way for you
to win too. But the reality is, that person did it their
own way, which is exactly what you should be doing.

When I decided to drop out of college and chase
my dreams, nobody in Miami was talking the biggest
boss shit that I was bringing to the table. Hip-hop in
Miami got its start with the up-tempo party music of
Uncle Luke and 2 Live Crew. JT Money and Poison
Clan took the booty-shaking music out of the clubs
and brought it to the streets. Eventually they passed
the baton to Trick Daddy, who put on for the Chevy
riders in Liberty City. I was something totally different. I was a nigga talking about $500 Prada sneakers
and trying to get a million. My music painted a picture that went way beyond South Florida. And for ten
years, I can tell you that nobody was fucking with it.

There was no love for what I was doing. As discouraging and frustrating as that was at times, at least I was doing me. I never questioned my vision and decided to rap like someone else instead. My city couldn't see it yet, but that was just because I was ahead of my time. I knew eventually everyone would come around. And eventually they did.

Stay true to yourself. Success is a long, hard road, and if the path you're taking doesn't sit right with your soul, it's harder to stay committed to the process. When you feel like you're doing what you're supposed to be doing, it's easier. I might not be a billionaire just yet, but what I do works for me. I'd rather hustle my own way.

Before we parted ways, I made sure to handle my business. I'd listened to all of Kanye's lectures and nodded my head in approval the whole time. Now he needed to hear me out.

"Look, everything you said is real good," I told him. "God bless us all. But listen, I need the beats."

"Oh, well, I've got beats, but what *I* need is raps written," he said. "So let's swap it out. The thing with these writers, Rozay, is that they can't write like you because they haven't lived the life to be able to understand my perspective. That's why I need you."

"That's too easy," I told him. "But I need my beats now. And the weird foam slides in every color. Size 12."

CHAPTER

20

NEVER LAY YOUR JESUS PIECE FACEDOWN

They say I'm getting money, must be illuminati
Talking to the Holy Ghost, in my Bugatti
He knocking on the door, don't let the Devil in
He knocking on the door, don't let the Devil in

—Rick Ross, "Holy Ghost," *Rich Forever* (2012)

HALLOWEEN WAS COMING UP. I WONDERED if the youngsters were going to trick-or-treat this year. It most definitely didn't seem safe yet. Cases of the fungus were on the rise and a vaccine was still months away. I couldn't imagine people would feel comfortable opening up their doors to strangers.

When I was a jit, a lot of people wouldn't open their doors on Halloween. But for different reasons. There were plenty of home invasions going on in the city. A stranger in a mask put people on high alert. These days you wouldn't let someone inside your crib unless they had a mask on. Ain't that some shit?

What some of my neighbors did do was leave a bowl full of candy outside their front door. The kids I used to go trick-or-treating with were real grimy street niggas, but one thing we never did was flip those bowls over and empty everything into our pillowcases. We never took more than one or two pieces of candy. Even as kids, there was a certain code of principles that we lived by.

In life you are going to be presented with opportunities to benefit yourself by way of fucking someone else over. I'm not talking about someone who you're in direct competition with. War is war and to the victor go the spoils. What I'm talking about is taking advantage of people who mean no harm to you. I'm about my paper and I want every bag with my name on it, but if it's not mine, I don't want it. You can't put a price on having a clean heart and pure intentions.

In my younger days, I got money in the streets. I can say that legal paper feels a lot better than the brown paper bag money. For a few reasons. The first one is obvious. You usually don't have to worry about getting locked up or killed over legal money. You can buy things freely with it. You don't have to hide it from the IRS. The second reason has more to do with the spiritual toll that ill-gotten gains take on your soul. The worst part about getting money in the streets is that a lot of times it comes at the expense of someone else's suffering. Somebody you robbed. Somebody whose corner you took. Or somebody whose addiction you took advantage of.

I remember back in the day when I used to move heroin and I could see the effects of it written all over the dope fiends' faces. That took something out of me. Profitable or not, I didn't feel good about what I was doing. At that time, I felt like I didn't have any other options. I felt that this was something I needed to do to survive. But I've gotten myself to a point where I don't need to make those types of trade-offs and accept blood money.

As tempting as those opportunities might be, you don't want blood money. That type of success is cursed. It's not worth having to look over your shoulder every day until a person you fucked over comes back to get even. Even if they pose no threat to you and you could easily squash them. Because if you believe in a higher power, and I do, you're going to have to repay that debt one day, whether it's in this world or the next one.

In 2017 I released a record called "Idols Become Rivals," where I called out the alleged business practices of Bryan "Birdman" Williams. The blogs called it a diss record, but I never really viewed it that way. I just had the courage to take a stand and put on wax what everyone else was thinking but was afraid to say. "Idols Become Rivals" was my response to seeing Lil Wayne's ongoing legal battle against Birdman and Cash Money Records. According to his lawsuit, Wayne had been cheated out of tens of millions of dollars he was owed in unpaid advances and album royalties.

Considering how much money Wayne had earned Cash Money for twenty years, it was unbelievable that Stunna could do that to someone he claimed was his "son." At the same time, it was believable because I'd seen so many other artists and producers make the same claim for years. It broke my heart because I idolized Birdman growing up. But I couldn't deny what I was seeing. In my opinion, the man let greed get the better of him. He succumbed to the temptation of blood money.

You would give us self-esteem and motivate our drive
But was in our pockets by the time we count to five
I pray you find the kindness in your heart for Wayne
His entire life, he gave you what there was to gain
I watched this whole debacle, so I'm part to blame
Last request, can all producers please get paid?

—Rick Ross, "Idols Become Rivals,"
Rather You Than Me (2017)

As the CEO of a label myself, I know all the little tricks and loopholes I could use to run up fees against my own artists. I never did any of that shit. Not every artist I signed to MMG lived up to their full potential, but show me one who blamed me and said I withheld money they were owed or that I kept them locked up in a shitty deal. You can't find one. Why not? Frustrated artists bucking against their labels is common in the music industry, especially in hip-hop. I've been one of those artists. So after all these years, why hasn't anyone ever claimed Rozay did them dirty? The simplest answer I can give is that it wouldn't be true. I can say that because I know I gave every artist I ever signed much more than I was ever given.

I never signed an artist and then sat back and waited

to see how I could make money off them. I flew them out to every city I went to so they could turn my fans into theirs. I let them stay in my homes for months on end. I sat with them in the studio and worked with them on their verses and hooks. I plugged them in with every artist I was working with. I leveraged my spotlight to shine a light on them at every opportunity.

The reason you don't see MMG artists bucking is the same reason you don't see niggas in my city bucking. It's the reason I can pull up to a trap in Carol City right now and niggas will run up on me like I'm the ice cream man to show me love. That comes from being a solid person.

You don't have to sacrifice your morals to become successful. I never wanted success that came from taking advantage of people. That's bad business. The temptation of blood money is the Devil knocking on your door. Don't let him in. Never lay your Jesus piece facedown.

CHAPTER
21

MASTER THE ART
OF THE L

THE PRESIDENTIAL ELECTION FINALLY WENT down, and Joe Biden came out of it the winner. Generally speaking, I try to take a back seat and listen more than I talk when it comes to politics. I have my beliefs, but I don't like to speak as an authority on things that aren't my area of expertise. I was happy to see Donald Trump out of the White House, but that had a lot more to do with his personality than his policies.

The events of 2020 had made it clear that there was a lot of change that needed to take place in this country. But neither one of the candidates had convinced me that they were the one who was going to bring it. I guess we'll just have to wait and see what happens.

People look to celebrities to speak on important issues, but the truth is, I have no idea what the answers are to all the problems that plague our country. Don't get me fucked-up. I'm not indifferent to these things. I have very strong feelings about what happened to George Floyd. In the days following his murder, I wrote a record called "Pinned to the Cross," where I tried to paint a picture of the civil unrest that was happening and of my experience living as a Black man in America.

But me writing "Pinned to the Cross" and having the words *Black Lives Matter* spray-painted on my basketball court weren't real solutions. They were just artistic expressions of my emotions. What people really needed to hear was a concrete plan for action from the experts on these issues. Everybody was posting black boxes to their IG for "Blackout Tuesday" and talking about defunding the police departments, but I didn't know what I was supposed to do with that. I wanted to hear what five moves we as a people needed to make that could lead to some actual meaningful changes.

There are people who have dedicated their whole lives to studying the issues of systemic racism. I feel my responsibility is to identify who those people are and to use my platform to lift them up and amplify their voices. Because the point of me having a platform isn't just so I can vent my frustrations. I need to use it to actually make things better for people. If your idea of success only benefits you, you're not really successful.

Anyway, I really didn't plan on talking about Donnie so much in this book. I had a problem the last time I offended his cult of followers. Back in 2015, I had a line about assassinating him in a song called "Free Enterprise" off my album *Black Market*. The next thing I knew, my album started getting pulled off the shelves of Walmart.

Inmates gave me commissary just because I'm famous
Or is it cause I'm rich and I know what pain is?
Assassinate Trump like I'm Zimmerman
Now accept these words as if they came from Eminem

—Rick Ross, "Free Enterprise," *Black Market* (2015)

But Donnie left me with no choice. If he had accepted his defeat and walked away with any remaining shred of dignity, I probably would have spared him here. But Donnie couldn't take his L. The man just couldn't do it. As soon as they called the election for Biden, he started ranting and raving on Twitter that the election had been stolen from him with no evidence to back up his claims of widespread voter fraud. It was pathetic.

I am a rapper by trade, and I pride myself on being a man of words. I can cut a motherfucker down pretty good with just a few bars. But let me tell you, I couldn't have come up with a diss record that was more brutal than what I saw Anderson Cooper say about Donnie on CNN.

That is the president of the United States. That is the most powerful person in the world, and we see him like an obese turtle on his back, flailing in the hot sun, realizing his time is over but he just hasn't accepted it and he wants to take everybody down with him, including this country.

Oh my God. The man just called the president of the United States an obese turtle. That imagery was immediately burned into my mind. An overturned tortoise kicking its legs in the air, trying to get back on its feet. As a fat motherfucker myself, I couldn't help but feel sorry for Donnie at that moment. How would I feel if someone used those words to describe my career?

> *The former Biggest Boss Rick Ross was once the most powerful artist in hip-hop, and now we see him like an obese turtle, flailing in the hot sun, realizing his time is over but he just hasn't accepted it. And he wants to take everybody down with him, including the entire Maybach Music Group.*

Oh my fucking God! I didn't even want to think about the psychological damage those words might inflict on Rozay. But Donnie had no one to blame for that spanking Anderson gave him because he brought it on himself. All because he couldn't take his L like a boss.

You have to learn how to handle losses. The sooner you become comfortable with taking L's, the better off you're going to be. Everybody comes up short sometimes. Everybody fucks up. On the pathway to success, there will be failures. There will be setbacks. It comes with the game. The problem is, not everyone has it in them to admit when these things happen. Instead they dig their heels in and deny reality, and nine times out of ten, it only makes things worse and more painful. More often than not, a person's inability to graciously take an L ends up being more embarrassing than the L itself. It amplifies the consequences.

I'd been thinking about this just prior to the election, seeing the situation with Tory Lanez and Megan Thee Stallion play out. I didn't know all the specifics about their relationship and what went down between them, but two things seemed obvious. First, that at some point, Tory Lanez probably had fucked up. And second, that the way he was handling his fuckup and refusing to take responsibility had only made his situation significantly worse.

I'd been in Tory's shoes. Well, I'm not sure I could ever fit into his size 7's, but you know what I'm trying to say. Going back to earlier, when I was talking about managing your emotions in stressful situations, I've fucked up, and I haven't always handled those situations the best way possible. But as I matured, I learned to accept my losses and turn them into lessons. It's not a loss if you learn something from it that makes you better moving forward. Then it's just the setback that precedes a comeback.

Here's an L I can take on the chin right now. For years I genuinely admired Donald Trump. I probably name-dropped him in my raps more than any other rapper.

Makaveli returns, it's God forgives and I don't
Resurrection of the real, time to get richer than Trump

> —Rick Ross, "Pirates," *God Forgives, I Don't* (2012)

Of course, that came from me being naive as to the type of person he really was. I just saw his money and fame and felt that was something to aspire to. But those bars didn't age well, and knowing what I know now, I can say he's not a person who should be idolized. He might be rich, but I don't want his type of success.

I think we all know when we've fucked up. Whether you did some dumb shit in a rage that you later regret or you were trying to do the right thing and somehow it went sideways, pretty soon afterward you know. It's that *Goddamn, I shouldn't have done that shit* feeling. At that point, what type of person do you want to be moving forward? The one who can own up to their mistakes or the person who can't admit to them?

If there's someone reading this right now who feels like they're getting called out, know that you most definitely are. You took an L by not being able to admit that you took an L. And guess what? It ain't a big deal. It doesn't define you or take away from your good qualities. You can work on yourself. Now that you're aware of it, you can do something about it. You can catch yourself the next time you're heading down that same path and say, "Yo, I'm doing that goofy ocky shit again. I told myself I wasn't going to keep doing this.

Let me stop now before I disappoint Rozay." Being in denial of your fuckups will only hold you back. Accepting your flaws and missteps is the first step toward making changes and improving yourself. At the end of the day, that's what bossing up is all about.

Taking a loss stings. It's not an enjoyable feeling. That's why so many people like Donnie just refuse to do it, even when it's obvious to everyone on the planet. They choose to point the finger somewhere else instead of looking in the mirror and taking responsibility for their actions. But the truth will set you free. So boss the fuck up and let that L burn. Let it sizzle like a cattle branding iron. Replay it in your mind over and over and figure out what happened and how it happened. It's the only way you can make sure you never make the same mistake twice and actually turn your losses into lessons. If you can't take the L, then you can't figure out how it happened. And if you don't know how it happened, then you can't do anything to make sure it doesn't happen again.

CHAPTER

22

YOU CAN ALWAYS
DIG DEEPER

Determined to be the best, not looking back at regrets

How many people you bless is how you measure success

—Rick Ross, "Shot to the Heart," *Trilla* (2008)

I LIKE TO START MY DAYS WITH AN EARLY morning barefoot walk across The Promise Land. Getting outside and connecting with nature awakens the senses. I always feel energized and focused by the time I get back to the house. Ready to take on whatever the day may bring.

Sometimes I'll bring my phone out with me and broadcast my "Barefoot Chronicles" for my followers. I tell them to rise and grind and remind them it's a perfect day to boss up. That, regardless of what may be going on, we're all blessed to have another opportunity to get closer to achieving our goals.

But on this particular day, I left my phone at the crib. With a joint between my lips and wet morning dew between my toes, I looked out into the distance and watched the sun rise. I took a hit of my swisher, and all of the events of this crazy year started coming to the surface.

How was it that during this period of solitude, living under lockdown, I felt so connected to the universe? How was it possible that I'd lost my biggest revenue stream but I was closing out the year richer than I've ever been? When I turned on the TV, it looked like the world was on the brink of collapse. People were still dying from the fungus. Protestors were in the streets throwing bricks and bottles at the police. The president's disciples were trying to stage a coup and overturn the results of the election. Everywhere I looked, I saw disease, chaos and destruction. But somehow I felt at peace. Everything was as it should be. They say God works in mysterious ways. God is the greatest.

I made my way toward the pond. As a kid, I loved going fishing. Me and my best friend Jabbar would fish out of the canals around the corner from my house. My daddy used to take me fishing too. I needed to get back into it with my kids.

I caught a few small ones, but my pond wasn't booming the way it needed to be. I wanted them to be jumping out that bitch. The fish in Ross Ponds needed to be in abundance. When I got back to the house, I texted my momma to find out what her favorite fish is. Whatever it was, I was going to get my pond stocked with those.

Later that afternoon, I reached out to some pond experts, a couple of white guys from Tennessee who had master's degrees in fisheries sciences. A few days later, they came to The Promise Land and spent a whole day conducting an audit on my ponds. Then they put together a fifty-slide PowerPoint presentation on the situation.

The Ross ponds were evaluated for approximately three hours. Dissolved oxygen levels were measured with a YSI ProODO meter; alkalinity and pH were measured with Hach strips; visibility was measured with a Secchi disc; 121 fish were captured via electrofishing, weighed and measured, and released. Following are management plans for both ponds.

The two Ross ponds are mainly limited at present by excessive shallowness, poor water quality and predator-prey imbalance in the form of low bluegill numbers. Once the two ponds have been drained and deepened to mitigate fish mortality due to thermal stress, they will be blank slates, ready for new stockings that will allow for quick development of topflight fisheries. Fish grow rapidly in newly stocked ponds; within two years of re-stocking you will have better fishing than what is now found in either pond, and two years beyond that you will have world-class fishing if proper management is consistently implemented. We look forward to helping you transform these two ponds into your favorite fishing holes on the planet!

The problem was my ponds were too shallow. The solution was to dig deeper. Something about that resonated with me.

From outside the gates of The Promise Land, nobody would be able to tell that my ponds could be improved upon. I think a lot of people feel that way looking at my success. But you don't reach life's finish line until you take your last breath, the curtains start to close and it all fades to black. Until then, you can always dig deeper.

I was getting ready to drop *Richer Than I Ever Been*, my eleventh studio album. It was the last album on my contract. I was going to be a free agent again. I had to deliver with this project.

When I started working on the album, the title was simply a reflection of my finances. It was the truth, but it was also superficial. As the pandemic unfolded, I started to have some reservations about it. Bragging about my fortune at a time when so many people were struggling might not be a good look. I thought about changing it.

But my experience of living through the pandemic had changed what the title meant to me. My definition of *rich* had evolved. It wasn't about hitting a hundred million anymore. It wasn't about hitting a billion. Spiritually I felt richer than I'd ever been. I'd done a lot of reflecting while I was stuck at home. I really liked the person I'd become. But I could still dig deeper.

The pond experts had drained the ponds—we found a few of Holyfield's old golf balls—and started digging when I announced a new venture a couple of weeks later.

I was making a $1 million investment and entering into a strategic partnership with Jetdoc, a game-changing digital health platform. As an equity partner, adviser and spokesperson, I would be using my platform to spread the word on the most exciting new offering in health care.

When I got the opportunity to meet with Tommy Duncan, Jetdoc's founder and CEO, we hit it off right away. We were both serial entrepreneurs who shared the hustler's spirit. We both had also experienced serious health scares at a relatively young age. Tommy suffered a stroke when he was thirty years old. I had my first seizure when I was thirty-five. Both of us lived busy, on-the-go lifestyles, and the traditional ways of accessing health care had never been a good fit for either of us. I can't plan doctor's appointments weeks in advance or sit in an urgent care waiting room for hours. Half the time I need to see a doctor, I'm out of town, and that means I'm out of network. So for years my hustle has come at the expense of my health. I learned the hard way that that's basically a deal with the Devil. It's not worth it. There's a price to pay for sacrificing your physical and mental well-being, and it caught up with me in a real way. I've come very close to death on several occasions. You may have read about a few of my hospitalizations on *TMZ*, but there were many more that never made the news. I almost checked out on you motherfuckers on several occasions.

I'm grateful I learned my lesson before it was too late. When I started eating better, exercising daily and getting more sleep, I was able to hustle even harder. I had more energy. My thinking became clearer and I made smarter decisions. My sex life got better. Every aspect of my life improved.

Without your health, you really have nothing. All of my possessions are worthless if I'm not around to enjoy them. You can accomplish your goals without running yourself into the ground. That's coming from Rozay. The biggest boss who told you to hustle hard every day. Hustling hard and taking care of yourself are not mutually exclusive.

What I liked about Jetdoc was what a convenient and affordable alternative it was to going into a doctor's office. I'm terrible at apps and websites, but even a tech-illiterate motherfucker like me could navigate this. It was obvious this was the future of health care. Especially with the coronavirus still going strong. People needed something like this now more than ever. A lot of people were afraid to go to a doctor's office in fear of getting Covid, and a lot of people had lost their health insurance because they'd lost their jobs. As usual, the people experiencing the brunt of the effects of the pandemic were black and brown. A tale as old as time.

Jetdoc was launching in Florida, before rolling out to other states in 2021. So this was something that could immediately help people in my city at a time when they were in desperate need of it. That was what was at the forefront of me partnering up with Tommy Duncan.

When people visit The Promise Land, they're always blown away by the sheer size of my estate and all of my possessions. I don't only have the largest residential swimming pool in the United States. There's another pool behind the guesthouse. There's an indoor swimming pool I've never been in. My bathtub is big enough to swim laps in. Go watch *Coming 2 America* if you think I'm exaggerating.

I like old-school '57 Chevys, and some of them I have three in different colors. I have one garage that's all red bones. Another one for the black cars. Another full of baby blues. It's the same fleet of cars. Just in different colors. I have a hobby shop that's full of cars I don't drive but that I just like to look at. I've got a white Ford Bronco just like OJ Simpson's. I've got a black vintage limousine. Old NASCAR racing cars.

As soon as you step foot inside my house, you'll see my trinkets. Piles of ornamental bicycles, pineapples and other tchotchkes. My walls are filled with art I've acquired in my travels over the years. There's a trophy room full of championship rings and sports memorabilia. Downstairs you'll find more classic video games than in any arcade that's open to the general public. There's another room downstairs lined with thousands of action figures and figurines from floor to ceiling.

I've been told that I'm a hoarder. Many times. But when I looked up the definition of the word, I didn't quite meet the criteria. Hoarders are embarrassed by their possessions. Their shit is scattered all over the place to the point where there's no functional living space left. Collectors, on the other hand, are proud of their belongings, and they display them in a well-maintained and organized manner. Anyone who has spent time around me—especially at the house—knows how meticulous I am when it comes to the placement of my belongings and how much I enjoy sharing and talking about them. So let's get one thing straight. Rozay is a collector.

Regardless of how you choose to diagnose my condition, I know that my desire to accumulate wealth and material things stems from me having grown up with not everything I wanted. I had a good upbringing. My parents weren't rich, but I knew a lot of niggas in Miami who came up with a lot less. But for whatever reason, my dreams were always so grandiose. I remember being a young boy riding in the back seat of "Old Scrappy"—that's what we called my daddy's Buick—and knowing that when I got older, I didn't want to have to manually roll down my car's windows. As far back as I can remember, I dreamed of having all the things I have now.

Once I became successful, I started buying everything. It didn't happen overnight. I couldn't get it all at once. Like I told you, empires are built brick by brick. But I finally got to a point where I had everything I had ever dreamed of. There was nothing left for me to buy. So the question then became, what was there left for me to do? Was it time for me to hang it up and just enjoy all my possessions? I didn't feel that way. Success can be a mirage. It's like as soon as you hit your goal, it's not your goal anymore.

In my first book, I wrote about how I no longer fear death, only unfinished business. Looking back on the events of the last year, I couldn't help but think about how it had started, with the loss of Kobe Bryant and his beautiful daughter Gianna. What hurt the most was how much they still had to give. Kobe's legacy as an all-time great basketball player was set in stone, but in the years following his retirement, it had become clear how much greatness he still had to bless the world with. In the brief second chapter of his life, he'd won an Oscar, published books and established the Mamba Sports Academy. It was looking like Kobe had another epic twenty-year run in him that might rival his first before it was tragically cut short.

I felt that same sadness months later when I learned Chadwick Boseman had passed away from colon cancer. I'd met Chadwick two years earlier at the MGM Grand in Las Vegas. We were both there for the Terence Crawford fight. *Black Panther* had come out a few months earlier, and I congratulated him on all his success. In my mind, I'd just gotten to meet an actor who would be one of Hollywood's biggest stars for the next thirty years. To know that he was fighting for his life and that his days were numbered fucked me up. He had so much more to give.

I still don't fear death. But I do fear unfinished business more than ever before. So these days I find myself thinking less about my income and more about my impact. What is this all for? What type of legacy do I want to leave when my time on this earth is done? For years I just wanted to change my life. Now I want to change the world.

Now that I have everything, it's time for me to make it all mean something. To use my resources, my wisdom and my story to help other people turn their dreams into reality. I'm just getting started on this next chapter. I've still got a lot more bossing up to do.

★ ★ ★ ★ ★